# "A Good Book on Sex"

By Brother Marcus and Sister Cecelia

Dedication:

"To my leader, teacher, and guide, the Honorable Minister Louis Farrakhan. We love you, and we only want to help you with our people. We hope that this helps."

Preface:

"We wrote this book because we need help... especially around sexual relations. Please enjoy!"

# "What is the Purpose for Sex in Marriage"
## by Minister Louis Farrakhan

In the Name of Allah, The Beneficent, The Merciful.

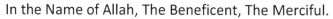

The institution of marriage allows the lawful sexual union between male and female in the eyes of Allah (God) and society. Since both, male and female should dedicate their lives to the Will of Allah (God) and the great struggle in the journey of the meeting with Allah (God), and, the great struggle of the union of the two, then the pleasure derived from sex is Divinely given to enhance the union as well as to re-charge the electrical energy of the male and the female that they might continue the great journey and struggle of life. These two, properly motivated, allows the sexual union to be a life-giving experience not only in procreation and continuance of the life of the species, but, it is invigorating as well as life giving to the marriage and the struggle of these two to become as one. To look at marriage as only the legalization of the sex act is to put our minds on a level that will not bring the best out of the experience. To become extreme in our view that the sex act is only for procreation and not meant by Allah (God) to give pleasure to married couples is a view that is not in accord with the Will, Plan and Purpose of Allah (God). These pleasure centers in the human being, used properly and in accord with the Will of Allah (God), brings comfort, ease, consolation, rest, reward and joy to the souls that are working hard to fulfill their Divine duty and obligation.

What is the purpose of sex in marriage?
1. Procreation of human species.
2. Reward the struggle of the two to become one with the joy of the pleasure of each other's complimentary nature.

3. To give rest, relaxation and new energy to the male to continue the great mission of being producer of mastering the earth and its laws as he strives to become Khalifah or one who stands in the place of Allah (God) at his level of development. The female in energizing the male and giving him this comfort, consolation; giving him peace and quiet of mind as a rest period between struggle is also satisfied and is pleased because she has given rest to him to work for Allah (God), her and the family. Therefore, she is rested in herself. This is the Divine Purpose of Sex in Marriage.

Satan, however, has taken this natural gift of Allah (God) and made mischief with it causing us to go after pleasure without struggle; without the burden or responsibility of being what Allah (God) created us to be. We have become pleasure seekers without responsibility and misusing our pleasure centers thus becoming slaves of pleasure.

This has given rise to the misuse of women and the misuse of what Allah (God) gave them for the man so that she becomes a prostitute – sex for hire, he becomes a pimp – using her and the need of the male for pleasure as a means of livelihood.

The lust for pleasure is causing the abuse of children, male and female, and the misuse of our bodies. As a result, we are living in a morally degenerate world. We are paying the price for this moral degeneracy through the plague of AIDS and sexually transmitted diseases, which produce the destruction of the male and female and the destruction of our future.

This is why we must return to Allah (God) and seek to know His purpose for what He created and use everything of creation in accord with His purpose for it. Then, and only then, will we find the genuine peace, joy, and happiness that we seek.
It is written in Psalms, "Behold, how good and how pleasant it is for brethren to dwell together in unity!"

The unity of the brotherhood gives us another kind of pleasure. It is written in the Qur'an that, when we become one with Allah (God) we will be well pleased with Him and well pleasing in His sight."

There is tremendous pleasure in being one with Allah (God). There is tremendous joy in knowing that we are pleasing in His sight. Let us strive for the real pleasure of life that comes from duty to Allah (God); duty to ourselves; duty to our mates; duty to our families; duty to our community.

Let us seek real pleasure that comes when we know that we have struggled to obey Allah (God); we have struggled to bear the burden of the great responsibility that Allah (God) has placed on our shoulders; we have accepted the difficulty factor of life knowing truly that after difficulty comes ease.

Please discuss this article with your family.
Thank you for reading these few words.

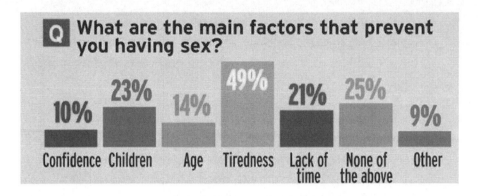

**What are the main factors that prevent you having sex?**

10% Confidence
23% Children
14% Age
49% Tiredness
21% Lack of time
25% None of the above
9% Other

### Tip #1

According to a recent **study**, your responsiveness to your partner OUTSIDE the bedroom can increase their sexual desire. For example, bringing flowers home to your partner after she had a rough day is being responsive to her feelings and needs. It's worth noting that responsiveness increases sexual desire for both men and women, but it has a more powerful effect with women. There are three ways that your responsiveness can increase sexual desire. First, your partner may desire you simply in response to being the object of your attention. Also, by paying attention, you might really "get" your partner, understanding their thoughts, feelings, and needs. When you convey a true understanding of your partner, they will probably feel more special, and in return, will feel more warmly toward you and have an increased desire for you. Finally, your responsiveness conveys a sense that you really care about and value your partner.

### Tip #2

It's not necessarily a full workout, but it can be as good for you as moderate exercise. It raises your heart rate about the same as a brisk walk or a slow bike ride. Are you in a committed relationship and finding your sex life leaves much to be desired? Tending to stress and relationship troubles is important, but if that's not the issue then it could be that your lifestyle is getting in the way. To boost your libido naturally and help restore harmony to your intimate life, use the strategies that follow.

Reduce, with the plan of eliminating, grains and sugars in your diet. It is vitally important to eliminate sugars, especially fructose. High levels of sugar in your bloodstream can actually **turn off the gene that controls your sex hormones**.

Eat a healthy diet, which will help to normalize your insulin levels. This simple measure has a profound influence on every area of your health, including your sex life.

**Optimize your vitamin D levels**, ideally through appropriate sun exposure as this will allow your body to also create **vitamin D sulfate** — a factor that may play a crucial role in preventing the formation of arterial plaque that is linked to erectile dysfunction.

Exercise regularly. Make sure you incorporate **high-intensity interval training exercises**, which also optimize your human growth hormone (HGH) production.

Avoid smoking or drinking alcohol period.

Be sure to get plenty of **high-quality, restorative sleep**.

Consider choline and vitamin B5 supplements. The neurotransmitter that triggers the sexual message, in both men and women, is acetylcholine (ACH). With too little ACH, sexual activity goes down. One way to safely and effectively enhance ACH levels in your body is to take choline supplements (1,000-3,000 mg) and vitamin B5 (500-1,500 mg).

## Tip #3
Helps Keep Your Immune System Humming
Sexually active people take fewer sick days. People who have sex have higher levels of what defends your body against germs, viruses, and other intruders. Researchers at Wilkes University in Pennsylvania found that college students who had sex once or twice a week had higher levels of the a certain antibody compared to students who had sex less often.
You should still do all the other things that make your immune system happy, such as:
Eat right.
Stay active.
Get **enough sleep**.
Keep up with your **vaccinations**.
Use a **condom** if you don't know both of your **STD** statuses.

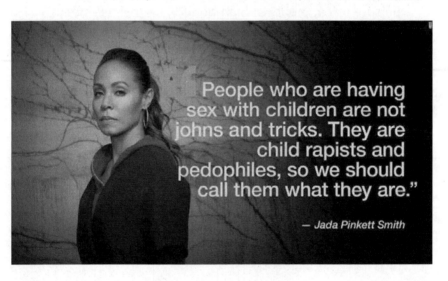

People who are having sex with children are not johns and tricks. They are child rapists and pedophiles, so we should call them what they are."

— *Jada Pinkett Smith*

## Tip #4
### Smile to Impress Your Partner
People start to get a sense of you within the first three seconds of meeting. Start off right by smiling. Besides making a good impression on your partner, it may also improve your mood and slash stress, boost your immune system, and briefly lower your blood pressure, too. Too often, we growl at our partners. Why not replace a growl with a smile.

## Tip #5
German researchers say the average intercourse lasts 2 minutes, 50 seconds, yet women perceive it as lasting 5 minutes, 30 seconds. Are we that good or that bad?

## Tip #6
Regular **sex** (and its primary side effect, **orgasm**) brings serious **health** benefits: It can cure **insomnia**, relieve pain, and reduce the risk of cancer, heart disease, **depression**, Type 2 diabetes, high blood pressure, bladder problems, and more, research suggests. Its power stems mostly from its aerobic element and **stress**-relieving effects. You can't be worrying about a problem when you're having an orgasm.

## Tip #7
One study of 112 couples suggests that moderation is key. A recent study found that couples who got it on twice a week had 30 per cent higher levels of an important bug-fighting antibody than did less sexually active pairs. But any additional romps—three or four times a week—vitiated the immunity boost. **Opioid** peptides, are released during pleasurable experiences. Normally, such peptides strengthen the immune system, but in excess they can act as immunosuppressants. It's unclear whether sex alone could amp up peptides to dangerous levels, but studies suggest a link between an excess of endorphins (an opioid peptide that increases during the deed) and depression, psychosis, and even immobility.

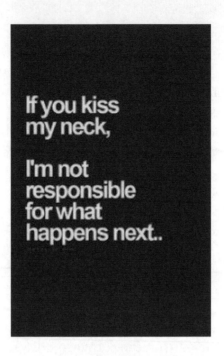

If you kiss
my neck,

I'm not
responsible
for what
happens next..

## Tip #8

Premature ejaculation is a problem that affects almost every man at some point in his life. There are primarily two methods if you want to last longer in bed: physical and psychological treatments. While physical remedies target the sensations you feel during sex, psychological solutions address your worry, stress, or other mental factors that may explain your quick trigger.

### Tip #9
Like the stuff dentists slather on your gums before jamming in the needle, there are topical sprays called "local anesthetics" that you can apply to your penis to lessen the sensation and keep control. When used properly, you can adjust the amount of desensitization with these sprays, and it won't transfer to your partner.
He says some of his patients have had luck with a product called **Promescent**. But be warned: The lack of sensation could make it difficult for you to stay erect.

### Tip #10
Smoking can shorten your penis by as much as a centimeter. **Erections** are all about good bloodflow, and lighting up calcifies blood vessels, stifling erectile circulation.

## Tip #11
### Boosts Your Libido

Longing for a more lively sex life? Having sex will make sex better and will improve your **libido**.

For women, having sex ups vaginal lubrication, **blood** flow, and elasticity, all of which make sex feel better and help you crave more of it.

## Tip #12

It's no secret that a man's sexual function declines with age. As his **testosterone** level falls, it takes more to arouse him. Once aroused, he takes longer to get an erection and to achieve orgasm and, following orgasm, to become aroused again. Age brings marked declines in semen volume and **sperm** quality. **Erectile dysfunction** (ED), or impotence, is clearly linked to advancing years; studies show that between the ages of 40 and 70, the percentage of potent men falls from 60% to roughly 30%.

Men also experience a gradual decline in urinary function. A man's urine stream weakens over time as a consequence of weakened **bladder** muscles and, in many cases, **prostate enlargement**.

And that's not all. Recent research confirms what men have long suspected and, in some cases, feared. The **penis** itself undergoes significant changes as a man moves from his sexual prime -- around age 30 for most guys -- into middle age and on to older age. Changes include:

**Appearance.** There are two major changes. The head of the **penis** (glans) gradually loses its purplish color, the result of reduced **blood** flow. And there is a slow loss of pubic **hair**. As **testosterone** wanes, the **penis** gradually reverts to its prepubertal, mostly hairless, state.

**Penis Size. Weight gain** is common as men grow older. As fat accumulates on the lower **abdomen**, the apparent size of the penis changes. A large prepubic fat pad makes the penile shaft look shorter. In some cases, abdominal fat all but buries the penis. One way we motivate our **overweight** clients is by telling them that they can appear to gain up to an inch in size simply by **losing weight**.

In addition to this apparent shrinkage (which is reversible) the penis tends to undergo an actual (and irreversible) reduction in size. The reduction -- in both length and thickness -- typically isn't dramatic but may be noticeable. If a man's erect penis is 6 inches long when he is in his 30s, it might be 5 or 5-and-a-half inches when he reaches his 60s or 70s.

An enlarged prostate gland can cause both **erectile dysfunction** and **premature ejaculation**. If you have an unexplained case of either, your doctor's looking forward to checking your prostate. Even if you're not.

## Tip #13
### Mind Your (Table) Manners

Put your best fork forward at meal time. Good table manners show that you're a class act and you think your friends are, too. Top table manners to cultivate include maintaining good posture, chewing with your mouth closed, using your napkin, and excusing yourself from the table when you get up. Thank your wife or husband for the meal and help out with the dishes. You will be so surprised by what helping your spouse out in the kitchen will do for you later!

## Tip #14
### Sex-Drive Killer: Stress

Some people do many things well when they're stressed. Feeling sexy usually isn't one of them. Stress at work, home, or in relationships can happen to anyone. Learning how to handle it in a healthy way really helps. You can do a lot of it yourself, and a counselor or doctor can also help.

## Tip #15
Explore sex together.
You are partners and you deserve to have a wonderful sex life. If you have any problems, or concerns you both are adults. You are both capable of discussing any sexual problems with accuracy and honesty. Be very, very, very honest about what you are thinking and what you are feeling around sex. Both of you have to and should be willing to work it out.

## Tip #16
If graying hairs, extra pounds, and dry skin make you see yourself as "old," you're less likely to see yourself as "hot."

Women may also blame menopause for lost desire when other health problems are the real stoppers. Common culprits: Bladder problems, an underactive thyroid, chronic pain, and medication side effects.

**What helps:** Get a checkup to make sure there's nothing else going on with symptoms that bother you. When you make time to take care of your body and relationships now, it pays off in many ways -- including more fun in bed. Your brain is one of your best sex organs.

## Tip #17

**"You cannot love a man that cannot feed love and make love grow, and love does not grow on sexual stimulation, Love grows by a man performing his duty, his obligation by that woman, and that duty is imposed on you by God, and the nature in which you are created, and that duty is to maintain her!!"**

- The Honorable Minister Louis Farrakhan

## Tip #18

Women and men can benefit from doing Kegels.
You've probably heard about the importance of Kegels more times than you can count. (But just in case, it's an exercise where women squeeze their pelvic floor muscles — the ones that can pause your pee mid-stream or help your, uh, grip strength — which tones them for better bladder control and stronger orgasms.)
HOWEVER, let it be known that men should be doing them too. A recent **study** looked at men who suffered from premature ejaculation. All but five of the guys who did pelvic floor exercises improved within a few months. In the male version, guys squeeze their perineal muscles (between their genitals and their anus).

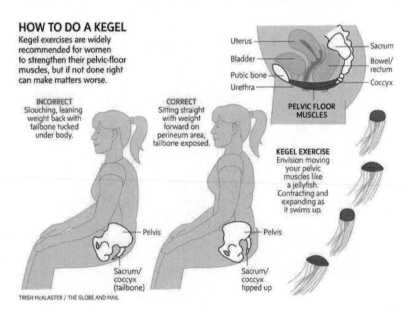

**HOW TO DO A KEGEL**
Kegel exercises are widely recommended for women to strengthen their pelvic-floor muscles, but if not done right can make matters worse.

Uterus
Bladder
Pubic bone
Urethra

Sacrum
Bowel/rectum
Coccyx

**PELVIC FLOOR MUSCLES**

**INCORRECT**
Slouching, leaning weight back with tailbone tucked under body.

**CORRECT**
Sitting straight with weight forward on perineum area, tailbone exposed.

**KEGEL EXERCISE**
Envision moving your pelvic muscles like a jellyfish. Contracting and expanding as it swims up.

Pelvis

Pelvis

Sacrum/coccyx (tailbone)

Sacrum/coccyx tipped up

TRISH McALASTER / THE GLOBE AND MAIL

## Tip #19
Sex is amazing for your health.
Consider it a naked cure-all...kind of. Research shows it can **lower blood pressure and stress**, lessen the intensity of **migraine headaches**, and give your **immune system** a boost. All good things.

## Tip #20
Orgasms do funny things to your brain.
In those brief seconds of awesomeness, there's a lot going on in your head. Parts of the brain associated with reward and pleasure light up. And there's the part associated with fear that tends to shut down. Recent research also looked at which areas of the brain are involved in which type of stimulation (like clitoral, genital, nipple, etc.). They found that the same areas of the brain light up in response to both nipple and genital stimulation — for both men and women.

## Tip #21
Improves Women's Bladder Control
A strong pelvic floor is important for avoiding **incontinence**, something that will affect about 30% of women at some point in their lives.
Good sex is like a **workout** for your pelvic floor muscles. When you have an orgasm, it causes **contractions** in those muscles, which strengthens them.

## Tip# 22
Keep It Clean
Scrub up! Wash your hands for 20 seconds before you cook or eat. Ditto after you use the restroom. It's one of the simplest, least costly ways to help avoid colds and flu all year long. No soap and water handy? Use an alcohol-based hand sanitizer. Be especially clean before you attempt sex with one another. There is nothing like hot, musty lovin!

## Tip #23

### Sex-Drive Killer: Partner Problems

Problems with your partner are among the top sex-drive killers. For women, feeling close is a major part of desire. For both sexes, watch for fallout from fights, poor communication, feeling betrayed, or other trust issues. If it's tricky to get back on track, reach out to a couples counselor.

## Tip #24

Switching things up and communicating openly with your partner can up your chances of having an orgasm.

Nothing is guaranteed when it comes to orgasms, but scientists have damn well tried to identify the things that will help you come. For instance, combining a variety of sex acts (like sex play with toys), along with penetration can make it easier for both men and women to orgasm, according to a study in the **Journal of Sexual Medicine.** Other research found that being in love or emotionally intimate with your partner can increase the probability of orgasm probably because it helps you relax and let go of your inhibitions.

There's research on heterosexual couples who were able to talk really specifically about sex. For them, getting super detailed — particularly about clitoral-focused stimulation (if they liked it, how they liked it, the speed/intensity that worked for them, etc.) — was associated with more pleasure.

Basically, science says that doing what you can to slow things down, eliminate distractions, and talk openly about what gets you off might make orgasms easier to come by.

### Tip #25
Using lube will help you have orgasms.

This is true for pretty much everyone, no matter what gender you are or what gender your partner is. Research from Indiana University's Center for Sexual Health Promotion shows that more than two-thirds of American **men** and nearly as many **women** have used lube. Almost half of the people who reported using lube said that it helps them orgasm. Hey, it's worth a shot!

**Tip #26**
Exercising can get you in the mood.
**Research** shows that moderate exercise boosts sexual arousal in women, and it can even boost libido in **women taking antidepressants**. Not to mention, exercise increases your endurance, alertness, strength, and confidence. It gets your blood flowing and boosts testosterone in both men and women. So if you were considering skipping a workout today...maybe don't?

**Tip #27**
It is your duty to please her booty!
Don't tell me nothing about I'm tired, I'm Sleepy, I'm fasting, I have a headache, I have to get up early tomorrow, I have to work the next day, I don't feel well, I have body aches, I'm sore, I'm in pain, I am under stress, I am too distracted, I won't do it because it would be bad for her health... I don't care what your excuse is! As the great Samuel Jackson said in one of his movies, "It's your duty to please her booty!!!" Especially if she wants you and needs you. Some of us as men are so niggardly with our bodies and with our physical presence. We hold back from giving her the love that she desires. Give her what she desires as best you can. She'll make breakfast for you!

### Tip #28

Some people can actually have orgasms from exercise alone "**Coregasms**" are real, and they're climaxes that can be brought on by ab exercises. About 10% of men and women have reported arousal all the way up to the point of orgasm while exercising. For men, it typically happens during climbing exercises or pull-ups, while women report experiencing it from sit-ups and yoga. It's something about the demand you're placing on your core abdominal muscles.

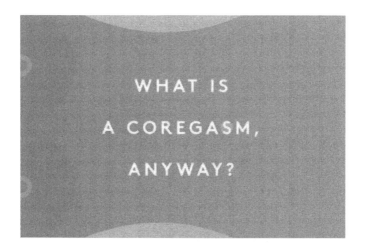

WHAT IS

A COREGASM,

ANYWAY?

### Tip #29

It takes two to Tango, and so too does it take (at least) two to make love. Unreciprocated love-making is unsuccessful love-making. The flames of love-making are quick to die when one gives oneself, body and soul, only to be turned away. Where the other seeks only a body, wanting only sex, love-making is squandered even if it is not (at least at first) apparent to the one attempting to make love. It is a counterfeit if based on pretense because there is duality, not unity, and there is manipulation and objectification, not authentic, mutual respect.

## Tip #30

Don't adjust your schedule just yet, however: Men who ejaculate the least (zero to three times a month) and the most (21 or more times a month) have the lowest relative risk for prostate cancer. The groups right in the middle are most likely to develop the disease, according to a paper in The Journal of the American Medical Association.

## Tip #31

Lowers Your Blood Pressure

Research suggests a link between sex and lower **blood pressure**. There have been many studies. One landmark study found that sexual intercourse specifically lowered systolic blood pressure. That's the first number on your blood pressure test.

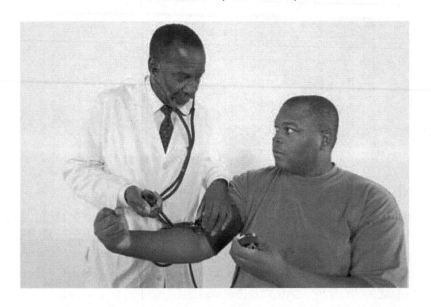

## Tip #32

Sex-Drive Killer: Alcohol

A drink may make you feel more open to sex. But too much alcohol can numb your sex drive. Being drunk can also be a turn-off for your partner. If you have trouble drinking less, seek help.

## Tip #33

Foreplay

The Urban Dictionary describes foreplay as touching / kissing / licking each other in a stimulating manner, in order to become "turned on" before having actual sex.

Foreplay is about touching and feeling your partner's essence. It involves their entire body, as well as their mind. Don't get us wrong: Chances are there are tons of things you already do to them that they love, and luckily for you, none of them require you to be a rocket scientist to figure out.

An important thing to keep in mind is that the best foreplay is not necessarily original or adventurous, but it is done with full attention to the job at hand (or mouth for that matter). It requires real time and real patience. Husbands I can guarantee you this. If you take care of her she will take care of you.

## foreplay

In human sexual behavior, the acts at the beginning of a sexual encounter that serve to build up sexual arousal, sometimes in preparation for sexual intercourse or another act meant to bring about orgasm.

# Ten hot spots on her body–and yours

Men and women ranked each of their body parts on a scale of 1-10 (10 being the *most arousing*). Check out how these chart-topping results scored

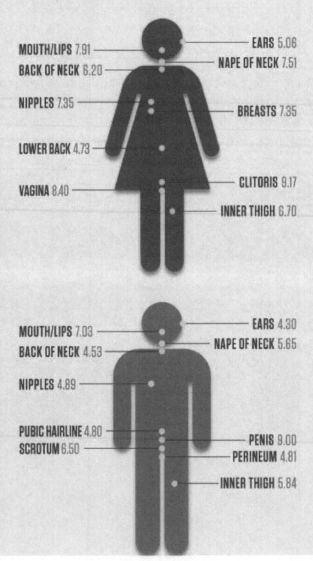

MOUTH/LIPS 7.91
BACK OF NECK 6.20
NIPPLES 7.35
LOWER BACK 4.73
VAGINA 8.40

EARS 5.06
NAPE OF NECK 7.51
BREASTS 7.35
CLITORIS 9.17
INNER THIGH 6.70

MOUTH/LIPS 7.03
BACK OF NECK 4.53
NIPPLES 4.89
PUBIC HAIRLINE 4.80
SCROTUM 6.50

EARS 4.30
NAPE OF NECK 5.65
PENIS 9.00
PERINEUM 4.81
INNER THIGH 5.84

## Tip #34

Lots of people screw up their birth control, even if they're trying so hard to do it right.

If you're using condoms plus another highly effective birth control method (like the Pill, the IUD, the ring, etc.), good for you! That means you're protecting yourself against unplanned pregnancy and STDs. A recent **study** found that about 12% of people did this the last time they had sex...but unfortunately only 59% of them did it correctly. The rest either took the condom off early or put it on after they started having sex. And since many STDs are transmitted via any skin-to-skin contact, that mistake is basically the same as not using a condom at all. So if you're going to double up, do it the right way and keep the rubber on the whole time you're having sex.

## Tip #35

Lots of orgasms a month can lower the risk of prostate cancer. This obviously applies to people who, you know, have prostates to being with. **Research shows** that men who ejaculated 21 or more times per month had a lower risk of prostate cancer than men who only came four to seven times a month.

### *Prostate Cancer*

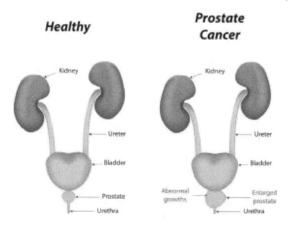

## Tip #36

"**70% of all women** need clitoral stimulation to achieve orgasm." Now, the question becomes where is the clitoris and how do we stimulate it? We have to learn how to satisfy our wives if we are going to be able to match them. So we have to be able to study the anatomy of the female if we want to be successful.

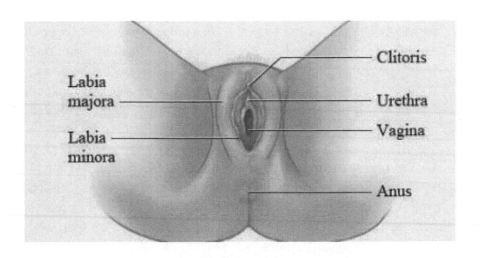

## Tip #37

Myth: Sex Starts in the Bedroom

Men may turn on like a light, but for women, arousal doesn't happen so fast. Pave the way during the day by hugging, **kissing**, and holding hands. Have some fun together, and show you appreciate her.

Feeling safe and secure in the relationship is key for a woman to really let loose during sex. A long hug can go further than you'd think. Hugging for 30 seconds stimulates oxytocin, the hormone in women that creates [a] sense of connection and trust.

## Tip #38
Myth: Assume You Know What your Spouse Wants

Just as many couples are faking orgasm today as 20 or 30 years ago. So, if your spouse is not enjoying themselves, you might not know it. Don't be afraid to ask questions like **"How does this feel?"** or **"Do you want something different?"** In other words, ask for directions.

## Tip #39
Stick to Your Plan

Don't think that if it worked the first three times, it will work the next three times. What turns her on may depend on her mood, and where she is in her monthly cycle. This plays a very serious role in sexual relations. Pay attention to your partner. Try different things and see how she responds. When you find something that works, linger on it. Women often complain that men move on to the next thing just as they really start to enjoy an activity.

## Tip #40
Counts as Exercise

Sex is a really great form of **exercise**. It won't replace the treadmill, but it counts for something. Sex uses about five calories per minute, four more calories than watching TV. It gives you a one-two punch: It bumps up your **heart rate** and uses various muscles.

So get busy! You may even want to clear your schedule to make time for it on a regular basis. Like with exercise, consistency helps maximize the benefits.

### Tip #41
Sex-Drive Killer: Too Little Sleep
If your sexual get-up-and-go is gone, maybe you're not getting enough sleep. Do you go to bed too late or rise too early? Do you have a sleep problem like trouble falling or staying asleep, or a condition such as sleep apnea? Anything that messes with a good night's rest can mess with sex. Fatigue saps sexy feelings. Work on your sleep habits, and if that doesn't help, talk to your doctor.

### Tip #42
Keep It Strictly Physical
Expand your idea of foreplay. Some men "focus on physical stimulation and often ignore mental stimulation.
While men get stirred up by what they see, women fantasize a lot during sex as part of [the] process of arousal. Be with your spouse during the entire sexual experience.

## Tip #43
Focus on Ringing the Bell

Most women need clitoral stimulation to have an orgasm, but it's more complex than you may think.

Some men don't understand the anatomy of the clitoris. It's more than the small "button" you can see. Its nerve endings spread throughout the vulva and inside the **vagina**. All are potential pleasure points worth exploring.

You can go back and forth. Paying too much attention to the glans, at the top of the vulva, can take away from pleasure for some women. It's so sensitive, that too much stimulation can hurt.

## Tip #44
"Not tonight, honey. I have a headache."

This old refrain makes us think of tired wives across the country turning down their desperate husbands for the hundredth time. However, the reality is that women aren't the only ones who suffer from low libido and lack of sexual interest. Men also suffer from low desire. And when they do, it can be incredibly complicated and challenging for couples to face. Many women feel ashamed and angry that their spouses are turning down their sexual advances. After all, men are supposed to want sex all the time.

It's easy to see how harmful gender messaging about sexuality can be, both for men and for women. Men feel overwhelmed that they aren't in the mood like they are "supposed" to be, and women feel suspicious and insecure that their partners don't want them anymore. They wonder: Is he cheating? Is it because I gained weight? Is he not attracted to me?

The reality is often much less insidious. Like women, men encounter low libido for a number of reasons, both physical and emotional. Perhaps he is suffering from a hormonal imbalance (men go through a "change of life" just like women do, when their testosterone levels dip), perhaps he is dealing with a chronic condition like diabetes, or perhaps he is simply too tired and stressed from dealing with work and his hectic schedule. All of this can do a number on a man's desire, especially if his relationship is tense and unhappy on top of it.

One way to deal with this is to consider his medicine cabinet. Did he recently start a new medication such as anti-depressants that might be doing a number on his libido? Other drugs such as Propecia (a popular hair-loss prevention drug) can also lead to decreased desire. Beta-blockers and anti-anxiety meds can have similar unwanted effects. He might consider talking to his doctor to find out if they are options that will interfere less with his sexual function.

### Tip #45
Another way to deal with this is to get exercising. Nothing is better for your physical health (or sexual health) than plenty of exercise. Take a long walk after dinner each night or join an intramural sports team together. Get active everyday and make healthy choices as a couple.

## Tip #46

Another way to deal with this is to encourage your husband to see a medical doctor. If he isn't interested in sex, it could be due to erectile dysfunction which can often be easily treated with medical intervention. Most men will avoid sex all together if they perceive any risk of poor sexual function and once performance improves, libido often follows. A doctor can also check his testosterone levels, which play a significant role in sexual function and interest and often drop as men age.

## Tip #47

Another way to deal with this is to address stress. If stress from his job or other aspects of his life are bringing him down, he might really need some support. Encourage him to reach out for assistance, whether that's from you, a friend or even from a therapist. In fact, according to the research, the best prognosis for a man's sexual dysfunction is when his partner is involved in the seeking of treatment.

## Tip #48

Another way to deal with this is to talk about it. Don't sweep the issue under the rug. If you want more sexual connection, you need to discuss it. Just make sure you do it in a way that is non-confrontational. Don't accuse him or insult him **("I can think of a million men who would love to have sex with me!")** Instead, say, **"I've noticed we aren't having sex as much as we used to. I miss being with you and I love our sexual connection. What can I do to help bring back some of the passion and intimacy back to your lives?"**

## Tip #49

Another way to deal with this is to initiate sex with your husband. Don't sit back and wait for him to make the first move. If you want more sex and romance, be the change you want to see in your relationship. Kiss him passionately when you leave for work in the morning, surprise him in the shower when he least expects it and be generous with compliments and positive feedback. If you make him feel sexy and desirable, he will automatically feel more in the mood as a result.

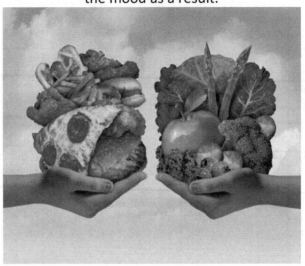

## Tip #50

Another way to deal with this is to help him to make healthy choices. A big hearty dinner with a few glasses of wine might sound like a good way to end the day, but it could also leave you both too tired and full for sex. Eat light, nutritious meals, and cut all alcohol from your life. Instead of zoning out in front of the couch, engage in some fun, heart-pounding (and libido-enhancing) date activities such as trying bungee-jumping or going to an amusement park. Push yourself outside of your comfort zone. The more you can get out of your rut outside the bedroom, the more you will get out of your rut inside the bedroom as well.

## Tip #51

If you're one of those husbands who thinks taking over some of your wife's household chores will translate into having **sex** more often, maybe you should think again.
A new study suggests the opposite may be true.
Married men who spend more time doing what many consider traditionally feminine household tasks -- such as **grocery shopping**, cleaning and cooking -- reported having less frequent sex than do husbands who stick to more traditionally masculine jobs, like gardening or home repair.
When it comes to chores, equality between the sexes doesn't necessarily turn on either the man or the woman, said study author Julie Brines, an associate professor in the department of sociology at the University of Washington, in Seattle.
So it's not sexy to watch your husband folding socks or unpacking the groceries? "While wives tend to be more satisfied with the **marriage** [when there aren't issues about housework], it doesn't translate to sex if the men help," Brines said. "For women in traditional arrangements, the wives' sexual satisfaction is greater. The wives are benefitting too."
In other words, even though women may say they like having their husband help around the house, his well-intentioned efforts may end up turning him into a helpmate rather than an object of desire.

## Tip #52

Lowers Heart Attack Risk
A good sex life is good for your **heart**. Besides being a great way to raise your heart rate, sex helps keep
your **estrogen** and **testosterone** levels in balance.
When either one of those is low you begin to get lots of problems, like **osteoporosis** and even **heart disease**.
Having sex more often may help. During one study, men who had sex at least twice a week were half as likely to die of **heart disease** as men who had sex rarely.

**Tip #53**
Sex-Drive Killer: Having Kids
You don't lose your sex drive once you're a parent. However, you do lose some time to be close with kids under foot. Hire a babysitter to nurture some time to be partners as well as parents. New baby? Try sex during baby's nap time.

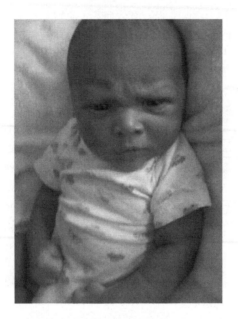

**Tip #54**
Helps Your Future Self
People who have more sex may have better quality of life -- and not just now, but in the future, too. If you have an active sex life in middle age, you're more likely to keep it up as you get older, which is linked to better health and happiness.

## Tip #55

Has your sex life become dull? Routine? As infrequent as a fair election in North America? You're definitely not alone: 57% of men in long-term relationships aren't happy with the sex they're having, according to a new Chapman University survey.

But it doesn't have to be that way. Another 32% of people said their sex lives were just as passionate now as they had been in the first 6 months of their relationships. The researchers asked them about their habits in and out of the bedroom to figure out what they're doing right. Follow their lead to get better sex—and more of it—no matter how long you've been with your partner.

One thing that you can do is to be affectionate all day long. The single biggest predictor of sexual satisfaction wasn't kinky positions or toys. It was how happy people were with their relationships outside the bedroom.

It makes sense: You're more likely to hop into bed with someone you're getting along with and feeling loving toward. So take the time to show your affection all day long—not just when you want sex.

## Tip #56

Another thing you can do is actually talk about sex. Fewer than 40% of the men surveyed had asked for something they wanted in bed in the last month. But the more couples broached the subject of sex—whether it was suggesting a new position, praising each other afterward, or asking for feedback—the happier they were with their sex lives.

If talking about sex feels awkward, start with a baby step. Say one thing you loved about your romp right afterward. Something like, **"It was so hot when you climbed on top of me. It drives me crazy when you take charge."**

## Tip #57

Another thing you can do is to **focus on her pleasure.**
One of the biggest predictors of a woman's sexual satisfaction is whether she's getting off. Orgasm wasn't linked to satisfaction for men, probably because it's a given for most guys. But the female orgasm is more finicky: Only 66% of women reported that they usually climax during their sexual encounters. It makes sense that if sex is more pleasurable for both people, they'll likely want to do it more often. And not shockingly, having more sex is one of the key drivers of sexual satisfaction for both men and women.

## Tip #58

They mix it up.
When you've had sex with the same person 1,500 times, a little variety goes a long way. Couples who tried little acts of adventure like new positions, sex toys, and wearing lingerie were more satisfied with their sex lives, according to the study.

### Tip #59
Set the stage for sex.
Lighting candles and firing up the John Legend CD can do wonders for your sex life. Setting the mood for sex with lighting and music was one of the strongest predictors of sexual satisfaction, second only to the strength of your relationship. It's about creating an intimate setting, which fosters romance.
And even though lighting candles and playing music is a total cliché, fewer than 17% of people actually take the time to do so. So be one of the people who bothers—it just might make the difference in your sex life.

### Tip #60
Lessens Pain
Before you reach for an **aspirin**, try for an orgasm.
Orgasm can block pain. It releases a hormone that helps raise your pain threshold. Stimulation without orgasm can also do the trick. We've found that vaginal stimulation can block chronic back and **leg pain**, and many women have told us that genital self-stimulation can reduce menstrual **cramps**, arthritic pain, and in some cases even **headache**.

## Tip #61

Sex-Drive Killer: Medication
Some drugs can turn down desire. They include some of these types
of medications:

Antidepressants
Blood pressure medications
Birth control pills (some studies show a link; others don't)
Chemotherapy
Anti-HIV drugs
Finasteride

Switching drugs or dosages may help -- ask your doctor about that
and never stop taking any medicine on your own. Tell your doctor,
too, if your sex drive stalls soon after you start taking a new drug.

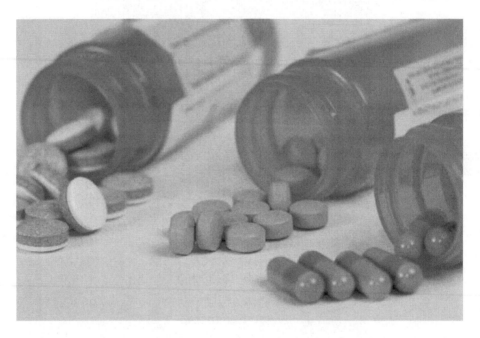

## Tip #62

Things That Happen To Your Body During Sex

The racing heart, the flushed skin, the complete calm (or the urge to nap, immediately) in the afterglow. **Sex** changes a person... at least for a few minutes. And not just because you're caught in the throes of passion, but because the whole process—from the inklings of desire to an **orgasmic climax** and beyond—is full of physiological reactions from your head to your toes (well, at least through your thighs).

Knowing these inner workings of your sex life may not seem like it matters much if you're happy with your habits between the sheets. But when something's off, that knowledge might help you pinpoint the problem. There are so many organs and systems involved in **sexual function**, and you need every single one to be in working order for everything to go well. It's not just all about hormones.

Here's what else is going on while you're getting it on.
Brain chemicals and hormones get busy.

Libido starts in the brain. What you might call **"being in the mood,"** scientists might call the right balance of neurotransmitters, like serotonin and dopamine, to facilitate desire. While the brain doesn't produce estrogen or testosterone, receptors for those crucial hormones are activated in the brain. Women's excitement phase is above the shoulders, versus below the waist for men. Which is why racing thoughts, **depression**, stress, or even just thinking about your to-do list are pretty instant mood-killers. As sexual excitement builds, adrenaline starts pumping, as do all three sex hormones. That's right, it's not only estrogen that accounts for your **sex drive** (if it were, menopausal women would be in trouble) but testosterone and progesterone, too.

During and after sex, endorphins surge, leading to feelings of euphoria, deep relaxation, and sometimes even less pain. Plus, there's that famed oxytocin, the so-called **"cuddle hormone,"** triggered by all that affectionate physical contact, which leads to feelings of lovingness, lower blood pressure, and less stress.

### Tip #63
Things That Happen To Your Body During Sex
Your heart flutters.
You're excited, you're physically active, and you need blood to get to the areas of main attraction, so your heartbeat picks up to pump blood around the body, with a specific focus on the genitals. Your breathing rate will increase too, to help your heart maintain this quickened pace. In this way, sex is almost like a workout and it's much more fun than struggling outside on a bicycle or running in the rain.

### Tip #64
Things That Happen To Your Body During Sex
Blood vessels dilate.
As your heart rate picks up, your blood vessels dilate or expand, which allows more blood to flow to those erogenous zones. More blood flow to the genitals is why a guy gets an erection and a woman starts to lubricate.

### Tip #65
Things That Happen To Your Body During Sex
Skin flushes.
Dilated blood vessels also mean more blood gets to the skin, too.
That's what behind any flushing, **blushing**, or warmth to the skin.

### Tip #66
Things That Happen To Your Body During Sex
Muscles contract.
Especially those in the **pelvic floor,** and nearby ab and leg muscles,
in preparation for climax. Your body tenses up before the relaxation
of an orgasm.

### Tip #67
Things That Happen To Your Body During Sex
**The vagina lubricates.**
Blood flow down below stimulates not just lubrication in the vagina,
but swelling of the **labia and clitoris**. This effect can be amplified
with direct physical stimulation to the area.

### Tip #68
Things That Happen To Your Body During Sex
Breasts swell.
Blood flow to the breasts can actually make them temporarily larger
and more sensitive. Nipples may also become erect.

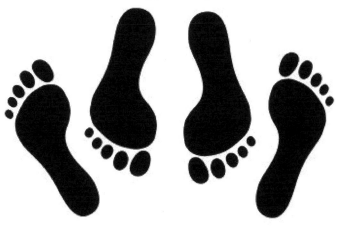

## Tip #69
Can I really break his penis?

Well, it's not a bone, but you can definitely injure it. It is possible to fracture a penis due to trauma during particularly vigorous sex. The erect penis is engorged with blood. Forceful bending of the erect penis during aggressive sexual play, can lead to this serious injury. Yikes. What should you do if you think this has happened to your man? Head to the ER! Urgent surgical treatment is recommended.

## Tip #70
Why don't I ever orgasm during sex? What can I do?

First of all, nothing is wrong with you. In most cases, this is just a matter of finding the right spot. Many women will not have an orgasm with vaginal intercourse alone and more direct clitoral stimulation from a partner does the trick. If that doesn't work, your lack of orgasm could be due to chronic medical issues (including diabetes, cardiovascular disease, and depression to name a few), medications like antidepressants, poor body image, relationship troubles, hormonal changes, or even stress. All of these things can affect orgasm and libido.

## Tip #71
Is it possible to pee during sex?

Not really. It's more likely that you feel the urge to pee, which is actually good news. This means your G-spot is being hit in the right way, and you might be close to orgasm. While it is possible to leak urine during sex, especially if the bladder is really full, we suspect this is actually not urine at all but rather female ejaculation which can occur during orgasm.

### Tip #72
How can you prevent queefing during sex?
Unfortunately, you can't really, it's just one of those natural phenomena we have no control over. Queefing is due to trapped air in the vagina and can occur during or after intercourse.

### Tip #73
Is it normal to get really wet during sex?
Yes, there's absolutely nothing wrong with a little liquid—or a lot. If you're having the opposite problem, grab some lube.

### Tip #74
What exactly is squirting?
Squirting is when a woman releases fluid around the urethra. This release is tied to intense G-spot stimulation. One thing to note is that it is not urine, though people often think it is. It's actually very similar to male semen, minus the sperm.

## Tip #75
What do I do if his penis is uncomfortably big (or uncomfortably small)?

Just talk about it! Don't be ashamed to address sexual issues, especially if you're in pain or you're not enjoying sex. If he's too small and is unable to please you during intercourse, there are obviously plenty of other things he can do. Let him know how good it feels when he uses his fingers or mouth on you, or how sexy it is to watch him tease you with his hands.

So what if the guy is too big for comfort? Use a lot of lubricant during intercourse, and go slow.

## Tip #76
May Make Prostate Cancer Less Likely

Going for the gusto may help ward off **prostate cancer**.

Men who ejaculated frequently (at least 21 times a month) were less likely to get **prostate cancer** during one study, which was published in the Journal of the American Medical Association. You don't need a partner to reap this benefit: Sexual intercourse, nocturnal emission, and masturbation were all part of the equation. It's not clear that sex was the only reason that mattered in that study. Lots of factors affect **cancer** risk. But more sex won't hurt.

## Tip #77
Sex Drive Killer: Poor Body Image

Feeling sexy is easier if you like how you look. Work on accepting your body as it is today, even if you're working to get in shape. Feeling good about yourself can put you in the mood. If your partner has low esteem, assure them that they're sexy.

**Tip #78**
Lowers Risk of Cancer
Men who have more sex may be less likely to get prostate cancer,
and women less likely to get breast cancer. Pregnancy and contact
with sperm may both be linked to the lower risk in women.

**Tip #79**
No touching
We borrowed this method from a Jewish marital tradition
called niddah. The idea is that when you're not allowed to have
something, you want it more. It's challenging, but it encourages us
to find ways to connect other than being physical. If you can abstain
for a week, trust me—you'll have that 'honeymoon' feeling again in
no time.

## Tip #80
### Improves Sleep
You may nod off more quickly after sex, and for good reason. "After orgasm, the hormone **prolactin** is released, which is responsible for the feelings of relaxation and sleepiness".
Orgasm triggers a surge of endorphins and oxytocin in both men and women, and that dulls pain and relaxes you. Both of those can help you sleep more easily, though according to scientists -- and many women -- the effect is more pronounced in men.

## Tip #81
### Sex-Drive Killer: Obesity
When you're overweight or obese, desire often dims. It could be that you don't enjoy sex, can't perform like you want to, or are held back by low self-esteem. Working on how you feel about yourself, with a counselor if needed, may make a big difference.

## Tip #82
### Play together
My husband and I make play a priority. I'm not talking about sex games—though those are great too. Tossing a ball around, throwing a frisbee, or having a pillow fight is a great way to allow yourself to let go with the person you love.

## Tip #83
Take a digital detox
Technology is amazing, but it can be a little all-consuming. For us, retreating to areas where the technology doesn't work is the perfect way to detox. No Netflix, no news, no social updates, no 'Pinspiration' means more nature, more laughs, and more sex. Plain and simple.

## Tip #84
Being Sexy to yourself
The number-one way to spice things up with your honey is by spicing things up with yourself first. Wear beautiful, well-fitting lingerie in the privacy of your home, just for yourself. It should make you feel like a walking goddess, and it will be your secret. Should your husband and you end up in an intimate situation later that day, you will already be feeling sexy, confident, and alive. And nothing should be more attractive to your husband than that confident, radiant feeling.

## Tip #85
### Massage

Make it a point each morning to give your wife what we call an 'intimacy massage' for about 10 minutes. It works best when both partners agree that it won't lead to sex immediately—it's just for intimacy and sensuality and can help couples reconnect through touch without the pressure to have sex, though it often leads to more intense sexual activity later.

## Tip #86
### Just do it

There are so many excuses not to have sex, especially since you became a parent: I'm too tired, stressed about work, or distracted by the demands of parenting. But just imagine you said yes! Just say yes whenever your partner offers or asks you to become involved in sexual activity. It will surely work and you will become more connected, have more sex, and get out of your routine.

### Tip #87
Candles, romantic music, and a good bottle of sparkling Apple juice are underrated, and using them is an easy way to make an effort and set the mood. Your partner will appreciate you for the effort.

### Tip #88
Approaching sex with the right attitude
**"You can mark your children with the way you think. And when the woman grows to hate you, she marks the baby with a disinclination towards it's own father because the way you treated the woman while she was carrying your child. This is why marriage is nothing to play with Brother. This ain't no sex party here! I mean you just don't get married to a woman because of sex man! You get married to a woman because you want to fulfill your life and you don't think about this being a temporary thing."**

- The Honorable Minister Louis Farrakhan

### Tip #89
Be Kind and Polite to your Spouse
It's basic: Being nice to your spouse shows them that you value them as a person. Practice being polite. Think about your spouse and what they have been asking you to do. Think about what you can do for them. They will notice you and you be impressed by you. Treating your spouse well has been shown to make you feel better about yourself, too. Prophet Muhammad said the best of you is he who is kindest to his wife.

## Tip #90
### Helps Fight off the Common Cold

Move over, vitamin C. Husbands and Wives who who had sex twice a week had more cold-fighting antibodies in their saliva than couples who had sex less often. Regular **sex** can help prevent you catching one of winter's most universal ailments – the common cold. Sexual activity boosts immunity. According to research, sex can lead to higher levels of Immunoglobulin A (IgA), which may offer some protection against disease.

This is however just one of the ways sex has been shown to ease the common cold; here are the others:

**Touchy-feely**: The sensation of touch during intimacy has been shown to have a positive impact on one's emotional well-being. So, having an intimate moment with your lover will help you feel more upbeat, and fight off any aches and pains you may feel from being sick.

**Better sleep**: When you experience an orgasm, your body releases a hormone called **oxytocin**, also referred to as the **"love hormone"**, and this can make you quite sleepy.

**Painkiller**: An article published in CEPHALALGIA, the journal of the INTERNATIONAL HEADACHE SOCIETY, found that the endorphins released during orgasm can block pain, even the pain of a migraine. So if your congestion is resulting in a painful sinus headache, sex might be a viable option for curing it.

## Tip #91
### Eases Stress

Being close to your partner can soothe stress and **anxiety**. Touching and hugging can release your body's natural **"feel-good hormone."** Sexual arousal releases a **brain** chemical that revs up your **brain**'s pleasure and reward system.

Sex and **intimacy** can boost your self-esteem and happiness, too. It's not only a prescription for a healthy life, but a happy one.

## Tip #92
### Sex-Drive Killer: Low T

The "T" hormone, testosterone, fuels sex drive. Testosterone may be the most notorious of hormones. It conjures up thoughts of muscles and masculinity. In fact, testosterone does fuel sex drive and muscle mass, but it also regulates mood and bone strength. When a man's level falls below normal, a doctor may prescribe shots, gels, or patches. As men age, their T levels may drop a bit. Not all lose the desire for sex as this happens, but some do. Many other things -- from relationships to weight -- also affect a man's sex drive and testosterone levels, so there's not a one-size-fits-all answer for every man.

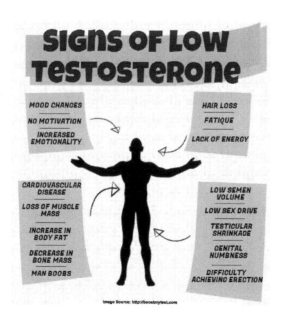

## Tip #93
Foods that may strengthen your Sex drive - Tart Cherries
How do you soothe sore muscles? Cherry juice. You should keep some at all times. The pigment in cherries and cherry juice mimics the effects of some anti-inflammatory medicines. And there are no side effects.

## Tip #94
Foods that may strengthen your Sex drive – Chocolate
Chocolate may improve blood flow if you eat the right kind. The flavanols in dark chocolate may curb levels of bad cholesterol, improve circulation, and keep blood pressure in check. Men with poor blood flow are more likely to have erection problems, so heart-wise foods may protect your sex life, too. But too much chocolate can lead to weight gain. Enjoy 1 ounce a day instead of other sweets.

## Tip #95
Foods that may strengthen your Sex drive – Turkey
Turkey is rich in zinc, which is critically important for the heart, muscles, and reproductive system. Zinc levels below normal are linked to poor sperm quality and male infertility. Not fond of turkey? Beef, chicken, and seeds offer a healthy dose of zinc, too.

## Tip #96
Foods that may strengthen your Sex drive – Avocado
Sure, this creamy fruit is high in fat, but it's the good kind. The monounsaturated fat in avocados packs a one-two punch against cholesterol. It can knock down total cholesterol and "bad" cholesterol (LDL), too. The trick is to use a "mono" fat instead of saturated or trans fats. And eat no more than 25%-35% of all your calories from fat. Olive oil and nuts also contain good fats.

## Tip #97
Foods that may strengthen your Sex drive – Fish
Fatty fish like salmon, herring, sardines, and halibut are another excellent source of healthy fat. They have a special type known as omega-3 fatty acids. These protect against heart disease, the top killer of men in the U.S. Two servings of fatty fish a week can lower your chances of dying from heart disease.

## Tip #98
Foods that may strengthen your Sex drive – Ginger
Slices of this spicy root are often served with fish or grated into an Asian stir-fry. Health-wise, ginger may help calm inflammation in the body -- which can come in handy when you push yourself too hard. Eating ginger regularly may help reduce the pain of exercise-related muscle injuries.

### Tip #99
Foods that may strengthen your Sex drive - Milk and Yogurt
The whey in milk and yogurt is another source of leucine, a muscle-building amino acid. We recommend Greek yogurt, with a thick, creamy taste that men may like better. It's also packed with protein, potassium, and friendly bacteria that keep the gut healthy.
**"Plus, it requires no preparation whatsoever."**

### Tip #100
Foods that may strengthen your Sex drive - Bananas
The banana is celebrated for its bounty of potassium -- and with good reason. Potassium is critical for muscle contractions and bone health. It also helps blood pressure. Getting enough potassium may be as important as eating less sodium when it comes to lowering blood pressure.

### Tip #101
Foods that may strengthen your Sex drive – Tomato Sauce
Tomatoes are rich in lycopene, a substance that may protect against some cancers. Some research suggests that men who eat tomato sauce regularly are less likely to get prostate cancer, but not all studies support this. Tomatoes have many other plant nutrients, too, that support good health. Adding salsa to a burrito or tomato sauce to pasta is an easy way to make a meal more nutritious.

### Tip #102
Foods that may strengthen your Sex drive – Mixed Vegetables
Vegetables are packed with phytochemicals, nutrients that boost cell health and protect against cancer. There are many different phytochemicals, and the best way to get a variety of them is to eat different colored veggies. There should be color on your plate at every meal.

### Tip #103
Foods that may strengthen your Sex drive – Orange Vegetables
Orange vegetables are an excellent source of beta-carotene, lutein, and vitamin C. These nutrients may lower your odds of developing an enlarged prostate, according to a large study. Good choices include red bell peppers, carrots, pumpkins, and sweet potatoes.

### Tip #104
Foods that may strengthen your Sex drive – Leafy Green Vegetables
Spinach and kale can help the eyes as well as the prostate. These leafy green vegetables have plenty of lutein and zeaxanthin. Both nutrients protect against cataracts and age-related macular degeneration, an eye disease that impairs vision.

## Tip #105
Foods that may strengthen your Sex drive – Eggs
Eggs provide lutein, protein, and iron, but you have to eat the whole egg. One yolk, with 185 mg of cholesterol, fits into the 300 mg daily limit for healthy people. You might also cut back on high-cholesterol sweets to make room for whole eggs in your diet. If you have high cholesterol, ask your doctor if you should limit how many eggs you eat per week.

## Tip #106
Foods that may strengthen your Sex drive – High-Fiber Cereal
Fiber may not sound manly, but it can be a performance enhancer. Executive or athlete, you can't focus on your goals if your gut is acting up. Fiber keeps you full longer and helps your digestive system run smoothly. This doesn't mean you have to give up your favorite cereal -- just try mixing in some shredded wheat. Don't deprive yourself... but add something good.

## Tip #107
Foods that may strengthen your Sex drive – Brown Rice
Brown rice is another great source of fiber, and it's easy to dress up with tasty, colorful food. Try adding lean meat, baby spinach, and pineapple. If you don't like the texture, mix some white rice with the brown. Brown rice and other whole grains can help you stay at a healthy weight and lower your risk of heart disease and type 2 diabetes.

## Tip #108
Foods that may strengthen your Sex drive – Berries
Berries can help you be on top of your game mentally as well as physically. They're loaded with antioxidants that may help lower the risk of cancer. Animal studies suggest blueberries can also enhance memory and thinking. Similar research in people is in its infancy, but looks promising. When fresh berries are expensive or tough to find, try buying them frozen and making a shake.

## Tip #109
Foods that may strengthen your Sex drive – Coffee
When you need a pick-me-up, we recommend making a good old-fashioned cup of joe. Research shows it can make you more alert, and plain coffee has almost no calories. This makes it a far better choice than expensive, high-calorie energy drinks.

## Focus on the Good Stuff
To change your diet, add good foods rather than denying yourself bad ones. As you get used to eating more fruits, vegetables, lean meats, and whole grains, these foods may come to replace some of the less healthy choices. Dietitian Bonci offers a sports metaphor to sum up the benefits: You'll play better today and stay in the game longer.

## Tip #110
Good for Mental Health
Adults in committed relationships who have more sex are less likely to be depressed or take medication for mental health issues.

## Tip #111
### Sex-Drive Killer: Depression

Being depressed can shut off pleasure in many things, including sex. That's one of many reasons to get help. If your treatment involves medication, tell your doctor if your sex drive is low, since some (but not all) depression drugs lower sex drive. Talk about it with your therapist, too.

## Tip #112
### Keeps You Lean

The more sex you have, the slimmer you're likely to be. Is that because more sex keeps you trim? Or because lean people have more sex? Scientists don't really know, but all you need is a partner and a bathroom scale to try to find out.

## Tip #113
### Sex-Drive Killer: Menopause

For many women, sex drive dims around menopause. That's partly about symptoms such as vaginal dryness and pain during sex. But every woman is different, and it's possible to have a great sex life after menopause by tending to your relationship, self-esteem, and overall health.

## Tip #114
### Be Prompt
Don't take a long time doing anything for your spouse. Being on time shows people you're in control and that you respect them and their time. Use datebooks and set pings to remind you of meetings and tasks. Prepare for big events and meetings the night before. Try to figure out how much time a task will take. Plan for bumps that might throw you off, like rush-hour traffic. Give yourself more time than you think you'll need. Be home, when you say you are going to be home!!

## Tip #115
So how do we compromise with sex when one person wants it and the other person isn't fully in the mood? Here are ways to 'do it:'

Start with communication.
**Communicate with each other** about the issue. This needs to be done in a careful, nonjudgmental, non-blaming way. What are the reasons that desire is down? Is it finding alone time? Does your mom-brain have difficulty turning off? Is it difficult to **get turned on in the same ways** that used to work like a charm?

## Tip #116
### Give each other options

This step is where compromise begins. If one of you has reduced your desire for sex, and the other person wants it three times per week, there needs to be a compromise. Can your partner accept once a week, if it means you can be fully engaged in it? That may not be his first choice, but **feeling mentally pressured into sex** can quickly build resentment and lead to even less sex.

Just by relieving this expectation so your partner isn't disappointed, you might feel more relaxed about sex and be more likely to enjoy it once it no longer feels like one more thing to check off the to-do list. And once you're more into it, that might make it easier for your partner to tolerate not having sex as often.

## Tip #117
### See a professional and use a few "tricks."

What if the desire to have sex just isn't there? First check with your doctor or integrative medical provider to make sure there is not **a medical reason that your desire is low**. But if that doesn't produce any answers, then it's time to pull out the bag of tricks!

Try some essential oils. Ylang Ylang, for example, seems to quickly bring a tingle sensation to the area where you apply it (Hint: on the inner-upper thighs—NOT right on your lady parts!). Dab a little on, and wait for the electricity to start.

Share your vulnerability. Men and women are wired differently. Men often like to have sex to feel connected, whereas women like to feel connected and then have sex. To get talking, try something like **The Ungame: Couples Version.**

## Tip #118
*How to deal with Knee Pain*

According to the American Osteopathic Association, about one-third of Americans have **knee pain**. Along with the day-to-day discomfort, that can really put a **damper on your sex life**. Here's the good news: Knee injuries and sensitivities don't have to put the kibosh on sexual intimacy—in fact, having sex could be beneficial for your condition. During intercourse, it may actually be helpful to move your knee through its range of motion, and the rush of endorphins could help you manage your pain.

If you've been avoiding sex because of pain or fear of aggravating your knee further, follow these recommendations from doctors and physical therapists so your **sex life has more ooh and less ouch**.

One thing you can do is to exercise regularly. **Strengthening your quads and hamstrings** can help stabilize and protect the knees. If you work out regularly, your muscles will be able to support your knees better during a multitude of everyday activities, including sex. Squats, step-ups, and straight-leg raises are **helpful exercises** for people with knee pain, because these movements help to strengthen the muscles around the joint.

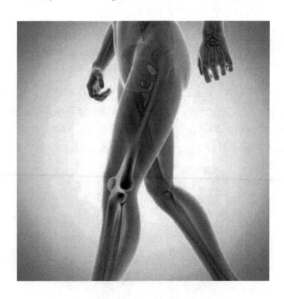

## Tip #119
### Another thing you can do is to take a bath
Take a warm **Epsom salt** bath before you're intimate. The heat may help proactively ease your pain. And, what's more, a relaxing bath is a great way to unwind and get in the mood—so light a few candles and make it a sensual ritual. Better yet, shower or bathe with your partner and make the experience part of the main event.

## Tip #120
### Use pillows strategically
Extra props never hurt anyone. Use pillows to cushion the body and to alleviate any stress on the knees. Place pillows underneath your knees, back, or stomach to help get in a sustainable, comfortable position (or **one of these that practically guarantee an orgasm**). Once you find one, try not to readjust too much.

## Tip #121
### Avoid putting direct pressure on the knees
If you've had a **knee replacement**, try not to kneel or put weight on your knees. The kneecap repurposing is made of plastic and is not made to have direct pressure on it. While it won't hurt you to put pressure on a reconstructed kneecap, it may wear out the plastic. If you haven't had a knee replacement, it still might be a good idea to stay off your knees to avoid the extra pressure.

## Tip #122
### Have morning sex
If you always have sex in the evening, try being intimate in the morning instead. Throughout the day, your knee pain can become increasingly worse. To lessen your pain during intercourse, simply try having sex earlier in the day.

**Tip #123**
Sex-Drive Killer: Lack of Closeness
Sex without feeling close can slay desire. Intimacy is more than just sex. If your sex life is idling, try spending more non-sexual time together, just the two of you. Talk, snuggle, trade massages. Find ways to express love without having sex. Getting closer can rebuild your sex drive.

> "You **must** reach out
> to each other,
> because if you fail,
> your marriage
> is doomed."

ELIZABETH BROWN

**Tip # 124**
Bonds You to Your Partner
The hormone oxytocin is released during sex, and it sparks feelings of intimacy, affection, and closeness with your partner. That helps build a strong, stable relationship, which is good for everyone.

**Tip #125**
Take Time Off
Take a break from time to time. It's not wasted time. It renews your energy, curbs stress and worry, and lets you enjoy and explore your spouse. You'll come back better.

## Tip #126
What can you do right after sex to boost your bond with each other?

Sure, basic **cuddling** and pillow talk after a romp in the sack can keep the two of you close, but word is that switching things up after sex can be just as beneficial (and a little more fun).
Any time you can inject change and surprise into your relationship, you're setting the scene for passion—not just companionship. By making adjustments to your post-sex routine, you may find that your overall interest in sex increases, as humans are naturally drawn toward novelty. More, passion? Yes, please!
To keep things interesting, there are things you can do after sex to increase intimacy, strengthen your bond, and make your next nookie sesh even hotter!

> Cuddling literally kills depression, relieves anxiety and strengthens the immune system.

Again, give your partner a massage!
Many of us use massage techniques **to initiate sex** via relaxation and physical intimacy, but giving a massage after sex can be even more intimate. Since you're clearly not using the massage as a gateway to sex, it's an opportunity to make your partner feel loved and appreciated with no strings attached. (Aw.) Bonus: A massage can also bring on the release of slumber-inducing chemicals, like serotonin and opioids, to lull your significant other into an even deeper state of relaxation (your baby may soon return the favor).

### Tip #127
Feed your partner!
Who says you have to eat fully clothed? There's a sense of novelty in sharing food between the sheets (and feeding each other in the buff), which can help take your intimacy to the next level. It's a super-sexy way to refuel.

### Tip #128
Slow it down
Using slow-mo versions of your go-to **foreplay moves**—such as light touching or kissing erogenous zones—can be a great way to bond post- Orgasm, as well. A slower approach to these behaviors can help you transition from intimacy expressed physically to intimacy expressed through emotions.

### Tip #129
Read to each other
More and more couples find that sharing a book and reading passages to one another helps them feel more intimate and connected. Reading the same book together also creates a common discussion point. This promotes emotional intimacy in a big way.

## Tip #130
### Breathe in Sync
Hold each other in a spooning position and breathe in sync (the big spoon can follow the little spoon's lead). Research suggests that couples' breath and heart rates tend to synchronize when they're close to one another, and some theorize that this can promote empathy and an intimate bond.

## Tip #131
### Give props to your Significant Other
Paying your significant other a compliment about the sex you just had, or about them as a person, can create all kinds of fuzzy feelings for the both of you. Obviously, showing your partner some love makes them feel adored and appreciated, but making them feel good brings you joy, too. (And you can thank oxytocin for those fuzzy feelings, a hormone that's linked to bonding and connectedness.)

**Compliments really *do* matter in a relationship—especially to people who tend to process things WITH THEIR HEART instead of their head or gut.**

## Tip #132
### Go for Round 2
If you're still feeling up for it, there's always room for one more round. Research has shown that both men and women are capable of multiple orgasms. While he may need a little time post-ejaculation, you can be ready to go right out the gate as a woman. Coach him into round 2.

## Tip #133
Your sex drives are out of sync
This situation can manifest itself in two ways: Either one of you prefers to get busy in the daytime while the other is all about nighttime, or one of you wants to do it all the time and the other doesn't. Even though it can be a real challenge, it doesn't have to be a deal-breaker. The best thing you can do is respect the fact that your engines are different and plan accordingly. See if there are cross-sections where your sex drives intersect, like doing it two times a week instead of either one or four. Or, if all else fails, be patient with your partner's **sex drive** to come around again.

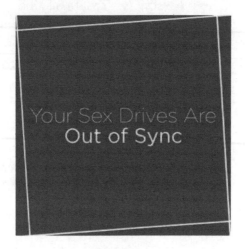

## Tip #134
You're not as turned on by your significant other as you used to be. It's supercommon for that **crazy-in-love early relationship** energy to wear off the longer you're with someone. The only time this is a red flag is if it makes it hard for you to be sexual with your partner. But if things are still hot, just not boiling hot, you're in good shape. There are plenty of ways you can heat things up again, including learning new moves and playing into each other's fantasies.

## Tip #135
Your sex drive tanks after having a baby
Having children does not have to be the beginning of the end of your sex life. Postpartum, your **hormones** get wonky in a whole new way, and the toll your sex drive takes is exacerbated by fatigue and intense focus on your child. Over time, your sex life will shift into a new normal—and if it doesn't, you can always get in touch with your ob-gyn for help.

## Tip #136
He loses his erection
When he loses his erection, many women feel like they're not attractive enough or that they're doing something wrong in bed. But that's not the case. Some men just get straight-up performance anxiety. Just have him focus his energy back on pleasing you, and it will relieve the pressure on him. Win / win.

### Tip #137
Your orgasm is ghosting you
There are plenty of things that can temporarily prevent
an **orgasm**—stress, an argument with a friend, even hormonal
fluctuations. Consider stepping up your foreplay game to give
yourself longer to unwind. The time to take action on this issue is if
your dip in orgasms is totally unlike the way your body normally
operates. If a few months go by and it hasn't come back—and there
aren't any obvious reasons for the shortfall—talk to your ob-gyn.

### Tip #138
Everyday Occasions That Call For Good Loving
Why wait for your birthday or date night to get busy? There's no
reason that sex should be reserved for special occasions. Not only
does waiting for the right moment put way too much pressure on
the event, but the more you get into the habit of having sex for "no
reason," the more you'll have sex in general. Win - win, basically.
Need some help getting started? Check out these totally non-
momentous excuses to experience pleasure with your partner
below, then get to it.

When your boss loves your presentation.
**Happy couples celebrate one another's accomplishments**, and
what better way to do it than hitting the sheets together? Don't
wait for him to get a promotion or for you to change jobs—make it
about the little victories.

### Tip #139
You see your spouse being good at what they do
Whether you overheard them on the phone talking business or saw them in action working with their hands, seeing the person you love at their best can ignite feelings of intense desire. So the next time you catch them "doing their thing," make a big deal of it by kissing them passionately, rubbing their shoulders, or just leading them into the bedroom.

### Tip #140
It's a Netflix night.
Whether you're watching Game of Thrones or The Bachelor, entertainment can be great inspiration for Making love to each other on a random weeknight. Use a movie or TV show that you watch together as a reason to bring up what turns you on—or don't say anything and just reenact your favorite scene together.

### Tip #141
You had a fight
On some level you know that those petty arguments are pretty silly. So the next time you're **bickering about whose turn it is to take out the trash**, redirect that feisty energy. The afterglow will have both of you happily doing chores and looking forward to your next chance to argue and "make up."

### Tip #142
The weather outside is frightful.
If you never thought the forecast was enough of a reason to get frisky, think again. Whether there's a blizzard, a heat wave, or a torrential downpour, use that time as an excuse to lock the doors, get cozy, and focus on each other.

### Tip #143
The kids are out of the house.
Whether your parents took the little ones for a long weekend, or your big ones went to a friend's house for the afternoon, take advantage of the alone time. Sometimes quick sex can be incredibly passionate, so make the most of your time.

### Tip #144
They look particularly good to you in what they wear
OK, so maybe your spouse doesn't look exactly the same as they did on your wedding day, but you have to remember there are probably plenty of times when you catch them looking super handsome, super pretty and, yes, downright sexy. Don't keep that thought to yourself. When you initiate sex out of the blue, they'll take it as a huge compliment, and your sex life is sure to benefit.

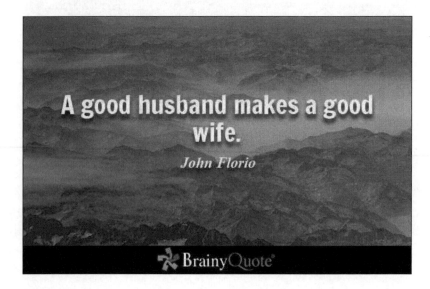

A good husband makes a good wife.

*John Florio*

BrainyQuote

## Tip #145

Laughter in the Bedroom is so very important!
The laughs we share outside the bedroom is one of the reasons why we have a shared sense of humor *inside* the bedroom. If you accept that sex is at least a little humorous, and if you and your husband know how to laugh together, it seems only natural to let some of that humor invade your marriage bed. So how do you introduce laughter in the bedroom?

**Laugh together, not at.** *First, do not harm.* You've heard that, right? So I figure it's best to start out with the caveat that if it's funny to you, but hurtful or irritating to your spouse — it's not funny. If you're the only one laughing, rethink the punch line. And insulting jokes — regardless of how cleverly you stated it — have no place in the marriage bed.

Above all, this should be a place that is pleasurable for both husband and wife and pleasing to the Creator of sex, our God.

**Access your innate funny bone.** Yes, you have one. Remember as a child when you had giggle-fests with friends and siblings? Or snorted at knock-knock jokes? Or did silly dances and fell down in fits of laughter?

Why did we stop doing that? What is it about becoming an adult that made us get so *serious*?

Sure, we see more and know more, and the full reality of life can make us contemplative and even sad at times. The Bible says, "For with much wisdom comes much sorrow; the more knowledge, the more grief" (Ecclesiastes 1:18). But even that same book says there is "a time to weep and a time to laugh" (3:4). So lighten up sometimes! Take some deep breathers and get yourself to the relaxed, welcoming state that encourages laughter.

**Laugh at your own bloopers.** Have you even seen the "blooper reel" for a TV show or movie? I think we could have one for our marriage beds too. Sometimes we have those embarrassing *oops*es where things don't quite go as smoothly as we'd hoped.

If you trip, stumble, say the wrong thing, make an unusual noise (yes, *sadly*, farting can happen during a sexual encounter), or otherwise do something that makes you or your spouse feel foolish, laugh about it — together. You're not on camera or being graded on a 10-point scale. You mess up, you laugh, you move on.

Make the mutual decision to give each other grace and grins when things go awry. With an upbeat attitude and a hearty chuckle, you'll recover and have a wonderful time.

**Be intentionally playful.** Bring your comedy act into the marital bedroom. There was a great TV show called ***Make Me Laugh*** in which comedians were given three minutes to make a contestant laugh in any way they could. For every minute the contestant lasted, they got a dollar. I still remember a few of the absolutely crazy things these comedians did. Maybe you could take a night and make your spouse the contestant, you the comedian, and see how long it takes to get them laughing.

Crack a joke. Wear a silly outfit. Do a crazy dance. Jiggle something (assuming, like most of us, you have something on your body that jiggles). Work up the craziest initiation line you can think of. Go for broke.

Get you smile on, and then get your sex on. (Which, well, *also* makes you smile.)

The point is that games often get you smiling, so feel free to play one in the bedroom. Get your kids' twister game and re-purpose it for a little naked limb-tangling, or grab the Nerf guns and have a foam dart battle, or play Strip ___. (*I like Strip Battleship — sink a ship, and your opponent loses an item of clothing.*) There are probably a hundred or more games you could play with your spouse in the bedroom, or simply buck naked wherever, that would get you both laughing.

And remember this is the best kind of game — where you "win" even if you "lose."

**Use word play.** This is by far the thing that enters my marriage bed the most, probably because I love a good pun. Now if I gave you examples, I'd be letting you steal our thunder — because hubby and I are pretty good with this.

But I suspect *you* can turn regular phrases into your own suggestive, sexy ones with a bit of imagination. It helps if you're willing to refer to each other's body parts in playful ways. (Of course, remember the first caveat above. And treat your spouse's body parts not just with humor, but with honor.)

### Tip #146
Make Eye Contact

It's not going to be weird; trust us. Locking eyes is one of the most effective ways to instantly boost lust. Looking at each other deepens your emotional connection, which, in turn, amplifies your arousal. Aim to stare into each other's eyes for a minimum of 60 seconds or throughout the entire tryst. Yes, this can feel intense, but stick with it. The longer you go, the more **bonded** you'll feel.

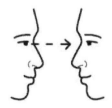

## Tip #147
### Do your homework

Sex doesn't just "happen," especially if you and your partner are in the midst of an especially long dry spell. About 15% of all relationships are considered **sexless**, meaning the partners haven't had sex in 6 months. Make intimacy a priority and sex will follow. If you're not currently having sex but are still being romantic—going on dates, holding hands, kissing—then it might be as simple as carving out some special time to be alone together. But if you and your partner have essentially become roommates, you're going to have to work a little harder to bring back sensuality. Plan date nights, start holding hands again, and give each other a kiss good-bye every morning and the romantic (and sexy) feelings might return.

## Tip #148
### Put sex on the menu

We don't just mean scheduling a regular romp, although they say that's a good way to keep your sex life alive. But if your goal isn't just to have sex but to make it more interesting, make up a list (menu) of everything you want to try and everything that's completely off-limits, then ask your partner to do the same. You might learn that you've both been fantasizing about adding **sex toys** to the mix or something like that.

## Tip #149
### Be a detective

What's really at the root of your sex issues? Figure that out and you just might solve your problem. Some patients have trouble initiating sex, talking about fantasies, or admitting they'd like to have sex more often because they grew up believing men and women aren't supposed to be interested in sex or because a past partner put them down. Other times sex problems aren't really about sex at all. If you don't trust each other or aren't getting along outside the bedroom, you'll need to work through that before you can expect the sensual side of your relationship to blossom.

## Tip #150

A sparkling **sex life** is something we'd all like to have, regardless of age. But as today's leading physicians and sex researchers are discovering, there's a profound link between the female libido and the constantly fluctuating hormones her ovaries produce. Find out how controlling your body's unique chemical balance—during every decade of life—can make the difference between a sex life that's so-so and one that soars.

### In your 20's
### The Advantages

At this age, estrogen, progesterone, and testosterone are at their highest levels. This biological bounce is an opportunity for lots of great loving—and babies, too. Because hormones surge just before ovulation, women are more likely to fantasize about and initiate sex during this 2- to 4-day window, according to studies.

### The Challenges

According to the 2010 National Survey of Sexual Health and Behavior, 20-somethings are less orgasmic than older women. Despite the hormone swirl, women in their 20s may not yet have the confidence to ask for what they want in bed, so they're less satisfied. Also, a recent study in the Journal of Sexual Medicine confirms that "the Pill" causes a decrease in sex hormones, especially testosterone, and so could lower sex drive.

## Tip #151
In your 30's
## The Advantages
A woman in her 30s may well find herself at an emotional sexual peak. She's clear about what she wants, even though estrogen, progesterone, and testosterone begin to fluctuate and drop off during this decade. More good news: Studies have shown that as women age, they become less anxious about their physical "flaws," which eases anxiety in the bedroom. The key is to think of yourself as a sexy, attractive woman, regardless of hormone tempo."

## The Challenges
After childbirth, testosterone falls to extremely low levels. For nursing moms, the hormone prolactin can suppress ovulation, as well as the production of estrogen and progesterone. All of that combines to make the thought of sex a big fat snore.

# Tip# 152
## In your 40's

### The Advantages

Female sex drive may actually increase as a woman's sex hormones and fertility decrease, according to a recent University of Texas study. Women with declining fertility think more about sex, have more frequent and intense sexual fantasies, are more willing to engage in sexual intercourse, and report actually engaging in sexual intercourse more frequently than women of other age groups. They theorize our female ancestors were so accustomed to losing children to disease, war, or starvation that they evolved to crave more sex at a relatively advanced age to produce more babies.

### The Challenges

By 40, a woman's testosterone levels will be about half the level they were at 25. And yes, that drop affects libido. For the average woman who enters **perimenopause** in her late 40s, fluctuating estrogen, progesterone, and testosterone levels may put a damper on bedroom bliss. To smooth things out, **Lubricants** and estrogen therapies can also help.

## Tip #153
In your 50's

### The Advantages
The middle years, between 50 and 65, constitute the apex of adult life. For women, the passage to be made is from pleasing to mastery. Mastery is right: The National Survey of Sexual Health and Behavior found 71% of 50-somethings said their last sexual experience resulted in an orgasm.

### The Challenges
Because of dramatically reduced testosterone and virtually nonexistent estrogen, **sex drive** drops after menopause. Physicians often prescribe very small off-label doses of testosterone along with menopausal hormonal therapy to boost libido. Also, the more body fat you have, the less libido-boosting "free-floating" testosterone you have. If you're obese, losing 10% of your total weight can do wonders for your sex drive, found researchers at Duke University Medical Center. Multiple studies have also shown that after just 20 minutes of exercise, blood flow to the genitals increases, resulting in more lubrication, better arousal, and better orgasms.

## Tip #154
10 interesting facts about sex

1. The word "clitoris" is Greek for "divine and goddess like."
2. The average man has 11 erections per day and 9 erections a night.
3. Scientists are unsure why humans have pubic hair, but they theorize that the hair traps secretions that hold pheromones, or sexual scents.
4. Avocados are known as the "fruit of the testicle tree" and are believed to have aphrodisiac qualities.
5. Having sex at least once per week can lower a man's risk of heart disease by 30%, stroke by 50%, and diabetes by 40%. It has also been shown that men with an active sex life are more likely to live past 80 years. [1]
6. According to the Kinsey Institute, the average speed of sperm during ejaculation is 28 mph.[6]
7. The amount of semen (from the Latin for "seed") produced with each ejaculation is 1-2 teaspoons. The typical man will produced about 14 gallons or 1/2 trillion sperm in his lifetime.
8. Many researchers consider the skin to be the largest sex organ and the brain to be the most powerful.
9. The black widow spider eats her mate during of after sex. The hungry spider can eat as many as 20 lovers—in one day.
10. According to the American Sociological Association found that the most mind-blowing sex typically comes with being in love with your partner.

## Tip #155
LOL: Laugh Out Loud

Laughing helps your body, most of all your heart. Research shows that laughter is good for blood vessels. This may help keep heart disease at bay. Enjoy a funny film or see a comedy show with your wife. Humor and health go hand in hand. Sex is very funny and should make for many memorable memories!

### Tip #156
Makes You Happy
You don't have to overdo it -- once a week is plenty. More than that, and the effect fades. But scientists only studied couples in committed relationships, so if you're trying to meet your quota by picking up strangers at your local bar, all bets are off.

### Tip #157
Practice heart breathing and soul gazing.
When you get into your heart space it will help you feel grounded and secure in the love you have for yourself, which allows you to **open yourself up to romance**. When you feel content in your heart, look into his eyes and smile. Lock eyes and stay connected with your heart, and he'll also soften up to be more open with you. When you feel comfortable together, it will help you open up sexually. Win-win!

### Tip #158
Sharpens Your Mind
Sex has been linked to the making of new brain cells, and that's a good thing. People over 50 who had more sex were better able to recall numbers and do basic math, and the difference was pretty big. It seemed to help men more than women, but both did better than those who had less sex.

## Tip #159
Build up anticipation.

Before you see each other, text them a couple of sexy messages. Try phrases like, "I'm so excited to see you tonight" or, "I remember the last time we were together and how you rocked my world." This will build their anticipation (and yours!) and they will be thinking about you all day.

Don't send him a 20-paragraph message because it will be way more fun to tease them and make them imagine what they want in between lunch and reading work emails. You don't want to be a complete distraction until you're in each other's arms.

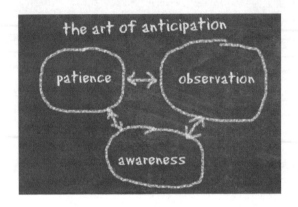

## Tip #160
Is your Weight Interfering with Your Sex Life

Cultural messages continue to tell us that no one bigger than a size 6 should be singing the siren song of sexuality. Much like oil and water, being **overweight** and sexy just don't mix. For those already struggling with **weight** and image issues, that powerful message can easily throw a wet blanket on even the most active **libido**.

People are internalizing society's definition of what it takes to be involved in **sex**, particularly the body shape. Certain physical conditions that go along with obesity also affect **sex drive**, further dampening the desires of those who are **overweight**. The good news: You can make some changes to your body (and how you think about your body) to enhance your sex drive. You can:

- Lose a little weight, even 10 pounds, to stimulate sex hormones

- Eat more nutritious foods, which control **cholesterol** and **blood sugar levels**

- Key your workouts to getting **blood** flowing to the pelvic area

- Pick up a sexy novel and start reading

- Accept your body at any size

- Believe in your sensuality

How to begin? Start by identifying the physical and psychological obstacles that could be standing in your way to a fulfilling sex life.

How Too Much Weight Hampers Sex Drive
According to a recent study, up to 30% of obese people seeking help controlling their weight indicate problems with sex drive, desire, performance, or all three. Often, the latest research shows, these problems can be traced to physical conditions that co-exist with obesity.

## Tip #161
### You skip pity sex.
This is also called "mercy sex." It's when you have sex because your partner wants to—even though it's the last thing you want. Some experts say you shouldn't turn down your partner. Mercy sex is acceptable on occasion, but a steady diet of it can tank your libido by training your brain to think of sex as a chore. It's completely fine to turn down your partner in a nice way if you're not feeling it. But if you do say no, try to be the one who initiates sex the next time to show your partner you desire him or her.

## Tip #162
### You know when to change things up.
Forget When Harry Met Sally. In the real world, it's hard to fake your way through sex. If you're not enjoying it, chances are your partner can tell, according to a 2014 study from the University of Waterloo, in the UK. What does this mean for you? Most couples find they get stuck in a certain sexual routine, and they may feel less interested in sex if it feels like they're in a rut. Although it requires a little extra effort, switching rooms or outfits or positions are all simple ways to make sex feel fresh again.

## Tip #163
### You're happy together.
It sounds simple, but there's a strong link between sexual satisfaction (factors like having interest in sex, feeling good about how often it happens, and infrequent arguments about sex) and happiness in your relationship, shows a study from Social Science Research. Relationship satisfaction fuels attraction, paving the way for better sex, the research suggests. So if you're into your partner, your sex life is probably in good shape.

## Tip #164
You've got a racy vocabulary.
Whether you're sending a flirty text mid-day or whispering something into your partner's ear, sexual banter is linked to greater sexual satisfaction for both men and women, per a 2011 study in the Journal of Integrated Social Sciences. Sex therapists call this 'simmering'—or little things you do to and for each other that keep you physically and romantically bonded. But this is just for your partner.

## Tip #165
You don't freak out about the occasional slow stretch.
It's important to have realistic ideas about what a healthy sex life is. Namely, it won't always be passionate and intense, and the frequency will ebb and flow throughout your relationship. If you accept there's no right or wrong way to be sexual, and you and your partner are open with each other about when you're feeling it and when you aren't, then you will have a healthy sex life.

## Tip #166

Think you know a thing or two about sex? You may be right, but you may also be way off-base. Read on to see what widely accepted "truths" can use a bit of a refresh. Once you arm yourself with this intel, put it into action—and you'll thank us.

**Myth:** Sex is better when you're young.
**Reality:** Sure, sex when you're young may be faster and more athletic, but most sexually active older adults report having the most satisfying, emotionally rewarding sex of their lives. There's less emphasis on quick orgasms and more focus on sensuality, creativity, and emotional connection. So don't envy the young too much—you could very well be having a much better time.

## Tip #167

**Myth:** Intercourse alone can bring a woman to orgasm.
**Reality:** Roughly 75% of women never orgasm through vaginal intercourse alone; they need direct clitoral stimulation. If couples want to climax simultaneously during intercourse, the best bet is for one of them to use their fingers or a vibrator to bring some joy to the clitoris.

## Tip #168

**Myth:** If the woman hasn't experienced a G-spot orgasm or had multiple orgasms, this is a sign of sexual inhibition.

**Reality:** Every woman is different. Performance-oriented goals to have the 'right' type of orgasm subvert healthy female and couple sexuality, and can cause secondary orgasmic dysfunction. Acceptance of the woman's sexual voice, including her orgasmic pattern, is healthier for the woman and couple.

## Tip #169

When your spouse gets you

**1. They know when to support you, and when to leave you alone.** There are times when you need them there, and times when you just need them to get the eff out of the room so you can have some space. It's important that they read the situation and knows the difference.

**2. They always knows the right thing to cheer you up.** They knows when to crack a goofy joke to make you laugh, or when you need to hear positive reinforcement, or when you just need some Chipotle.

**3. They never get mad when you criticize him, because they understand what you're trying to say.** You can say something negative without turning a conversation into an argument. If they are talking about friction with their boss at work, you can tell them he should probably start getting to work on time, and they won't go on the defensive. And they can do the same for you. There's a mutual respect and understanding when it comes time to be honest about the things that bug you.

**4. They doesn't try and change you.** They love you for you, and they understand that even your weirder quirks are what make you who you are. If you need that Instagram of your burgers before they are allowed to dig in, fine, they know waiting the extra 6 minutes for you to get the perfect angle is how they show their love. Sure, they might ask you to warn them next time there's a photoshoot so they can eat a snack first, but that's not the *worst* thing.

**5. They listen when you just need someone to listen**. They know when to just shut up and listen to you rant about work, or how you just can't afford to be a bridesmaid again and can't we just send them a toaster? Sometimes, you don't need to hear words of encouragement, and they can tell when you just want to vent. They don't need to fix everything to be there for you.

**6. They support you when you need backup.** More importantly, they support you with no questions asked. You're pretty sure he'd punch out his own dad if you told him he messed with you (but of course, you'd never ask him to punch his own dad).

**7. They trust you implicitly**. They don't frantically text you if you're out a little later than anticipated. They are not jealous of your coworkers. There are never arguments. They are confident in your relationship.

**8. Don't even try and mess with their gift giving skills.** They are the kind of guy who will own your birthday by presenting you with the perfect thing based on some off-hand comment you made six months ago about how it would be fun to start making your own this or that at home.

**9. You don't feel like you need to be constantly "on" with him or her.** With some people, you constantly feel pressure to behave a certain way and to meet their expectations. But you can let your guard down and be weird or cranky or tired with them. It's not even a question that you can fart in front of each other. If you're both still holding in your gas, there's a problem with this relationship.

**10. You can tell them anything and know they won't judge you for it.** You've told them your most embarrassing stories from the 5th grade and nothing phases them. There's really nothing you can't share together. That's the person that your making love with. That's the person you want to be with.

Tip #170
Sex is to a happy relationship what butter is to a summer whiting feast: totally and completely necessary. It's something you do with your partner that most people don't do with anyone else, so it sets the relationship apart and makes it special. Here, experts share the bedroom routines that separate the so-in-love couples from the rest.

**They believe in their sexiness**
One of the most important sexual habits happy couples have is assuming their partner is turned on by them. If it seems like a basic step, that's because it kind of is! It reinforces the feeling of mutual sexual interest. This is key because in Ofman's clinical experience, women sometimes discount their partners' sexual interest as thinking that's just what men are like rather than realizing their guys are specifically turned on by them. That distinction can make a world of difference.

### Tip #171
They don't underestimate the little things

Is surprising your partner naked and wrapped in fine silk a good way to get things going? Sure, but happy couples know they don't need to make a big production to keep things hot. A simple phone call at lunch to say, 'I miss you' can make your lover's whole day, a sexy text message can prime you both for an evening of intimacy, and a meaningful touch on the arm or even hand-holding while walking the dog can really restore your connection.

### Tip #172
They focus on the positive

Let your partner know what turns you on. Happy couples share what they enjoy in a positive way, rather than focusing on what they dislike or being critical. Even something as simple as, **"I enjoyed when you did such-and-such"**, can make a sexual experience better. It's all about positive reinforcement (unless something actually hurts / feels uncomfortable, in which case, definitely speak up). Even if a certain technique of his / her isn't working for you, redirect them by focusing on what would get you going rather than why their move is a total bedroom fail.

## Tip #173
### They make time for sex
If the new-relationship days when you were going at it like rabbits are just a distant memory, your significant other should still rank high on your to-do list. People feel sex should come naturally. It's true, it should, but we have a very busy culture where there's a lot of distraction and chronic exhaustion. If you have to schedule sex to keep the connection alive, so be it! Keep checking in with each other to determine how much sex you both need to stay satisfied, then do your best to make it happen.

## Tip #174
### They don't put too much pressure on themselves
Yes, it would be awesome if every single time was the way it goes in a romance movie: You rip each other's clothes off passionately, look stunning while doing it, then both get off multiple times. But real-life sex isn't always like that, and that's okay. Happy couples don't feel like sex has to be spectacular every time. It's not a performance sport. It's a mindful experience with each other. The pressure for every time to be perfect can make things worse, especially if you don't have a ton of sex. Think about it: If you rarely have sex, chances are it'll be harder to have a crazy good experience. That, in turn, could make you feel even less like having sex. Can anyone say **"vicious cycle"**?

## Tip #175
### They're responsive no matter what

That doesn't mean having sex when you don't want to! It just means not fully shutting your partner down when you're not feeling it. Happy couples are willing to be understanding and open about their partner's sexual desires, and they're responsive even if they're not necessarily always in the mood. Maybe they don't want full-on sex, but just to be held. If not, they'll make a plan to connect sexually at a later time or the next day. They don't just say 'No.'" Not wanting sex while your partner does is totally your prerogative, and vice-versa. Just make it clear that it isn't a rejection of your partner; it's just not the right time.

## Tip #176
### They're psyched to have sex

If you'd rather zone out in front of the TV than have sex but you do it anyway, your spouse can probably tell. That's bad news bears for your satisfaction, both in the bedroom and out. Nothing is deadlier than the perception that someone is only participating because they feel obligated. Instead, people (especially women) in ecstatic relationships get themselves into a frame of mind that focuses on how much fun sex is for them. Thinking about what's pleasurable or erotic for you instead of just doing it for him makes you more likely to have a good sexual experience.

# PSYCHED

## Tip #177

You know sex feels good and does wonders for your mood, but did you know that it benefits your health (his too!) in a number of not-so-obvious ways? The reason, according to scientists, is that during sex, our bodies produce a cascade of hormones (and other biological changes) that can ease pain, **lower cancer risk**, boost immunity, and even offset menopausal symptoms. Taking care of your health has never been so much fun.

It reduces chronic pain

Next time you have a headache, just say yes. Stimulation of your clitoris and vaginal walls triggers the release of endorphins, **corticosteroids**, and other natural painkillers. As a result, you'll feel less pain from headaches and sore muscles during sex. The benefit, which begins before you orgasm, can linger for up to 2 days. Research says that women could withstand painful pressure to their fingers while they were stimulated with sex toys; during orgasm and their pain tolerance doubled. And self-stimulation through the front wall of the vagina, where some find their G-spot, increases pain tolerance and pain detection thresholds by up to 50%.

## Tip #178
### It lowers breast cancer risk

During arousal and orgasm, your levels of "happiness" hormones rise. Two of these—oxytocin and DHEA—may help keep breasts be cancer free. One study showed that women who have sex more than once a month have a lower risk of developing breast cancer than those who are less sexually active. And Greek researchers found that men who had at least seven orgasms a month in their 50s had a significantly lower chance of developing male breast cancer.

## Tip #179

*"Talking about sex in general can feel scary or awkward. But learning to sit with uncomfortable feelings is a key adult skill."*
Kate McCombs

Intimate conversations aren't just about pleasure. Other topics about sex can include:

sexual health
how frequently we'd like sex
how to explore unknowns
how to deal with differences in what we and our partners enjoy

Talking about these topics can also help build a foundation for a better relationship as you learn about each other and explore new things together, all while being on the same page. It's also worth getting past the discomfort to talk about health, particularly sexually transmitted infections (STIs) and birth control. Avoiding these vital conversations might be endangering your health and altering the future you'd hoped for.

### Tip #180
Use a sugar-free lubricant.
Lubricant should be a part of everyone's sexual arsenal, but diabetics need to watch which lubes they choose. Some lubricants actually contain forms of sugar, such as glycerin and propylene glycol, which will throw off your vaginal pH and possibly trigger yeast infections. The last thing you want if you already have higher levels of sugar in your vagina is to add more sugar to it. Check the ingredients list and choose a silicone-based lube.

### Tip #181
3 Best Sex Positions For Back Pain
The best sex positions to keep the pain off your mind
Talk about a mood killer: Up to 73% of women with lower-back pain report having less **sex** as a result of their discomfort. Good thing researchers at Waterloo University ID'd the best sex positions to keep the lovin' alive (no ice packs necessary).

If your pain gets worse when you touch your toes or sit for long periods, **making love** in a neutral spine position is one of the best sex positions, supporting yourself on your hands and knees (not your elbows).

If arching your back or lying on your stomach hurts, missionary with a pillow under your back is one of the best sex positions so your spine is in as neutral a position as possible.

A general note for all back-pain sufferers (men included): When you're **controlling the motion**, using your knees and hips (rather than your spine) is one of the best sex positions to minimize potential discomfort.

### Tip #182

It's a common situation: What once was hot and heavy has gone, well, rather tepid. Most couples chalk this up to the natural progression of a long-term relationship. But it could be that your health habits outside the bedroom are to blame for your struggles inside it. People think sexual health is all about sexually transmitted infections and birth control. But our sex lives are linked intrinsically to our general health.

Here, the unhealthy behaviors that might be keeping you and your partner from the **best sex of your lives**:

1. You're not sleeping enough.

Up to 70 million Americans suffer from chronic sleep problems, according to the National Institutes of Health. The CDC has even gone so far as to declare insufficient sleep a public health epidemic. Not only does a lack of Z's leave you fatigued and prone to illness, but it has also been shown to have sexual repercussions—for both men and women, according to **a study** in Brain Research. How much shuteye do you need? The sweet spot is 5 to 7 complete REM cycles, or 7 to 9 hours per night. He suggests using the website **sleepyti.me** to easily calculate when you need to fall asleep in order to wake up feeling refreshed.

### Tip #183

Aerobic capacity and stamina, as well as strength and flexibility, are just as valuable between the sheets as they are on the streets in your day-to-day life. Research also points to the benefits of exercise right before you plan to get busy. Getting your heart rate up improves blood flow, which stimulates your sex organs. Any increase in exercise is worthwhile. If you add just a 30-minute walk a day or begin a yoga practice, you'll have better sex than before you started.

### Tip #184

You have bad bedroom juju.

You've probably heard you should make your bedroom a haven for sleep. The same goes for sex. If the room isn't conducive to intimate relations, you're fighting an uphill battle. You should avoid doing work or using your laptop in bed, clear the children's toys off the floor, and remove anything that keeps you from focusing on the task at hand. One brother told us that he has a photo of his in-laws on the dresser next to his bed. You want your sexual environment to be stimulating, not distracting!

### Tip #185
You're missing out on essential nutrients.
Eating a balanced diet ensures you get all the vitamins and minerals that have been linked to proper sexual functioning. Zinc is vital for male sexual health. He also points to the importance of B vitamins like niacin—found in salmon, chicken, and tuna—when it comes to energy production and blood flow, which are both important for sexually active men and women.

### Tip #186
Sometimes it's easier to give into your excuses—I'm too tired, let's just do it this weekend, it doesn't even feel that great to begin with. But we don't need to tell you that sex is essential for a healthy marriage—and also a healthy you. Research shows that a happy sex life can stamp out stress, reduce heart disease risk, and even improve immunity. But enough of the non-sexy talk. Try just one of these tricks today. You can thank us later.

Smell your way sexy.
Cucumber, licorice, and baby powder have been shown to turn women on, increasing vaginal blood flow by 13%. Pumpkin pie and lavender increase blood flow by 11%.

## Tip #187
Desire discrepancy

**"Desire discrepancy,"** is very common - but if ignored, it can wreak havoc on your love life. Is probably the most frequent complaint that you hear and it goes both ways. More often, the man wants more **sex** than the woman. But sometimes, it's the other way around, and women may feel embarrassed about it. Mismatched **sex drive** is the number one problem that therapists see patients for.

The good news: There is something you can do! Indeed, you and your partner can take steps to re-sync your sex drives, restore sexual compatibility, and rev up your **libido**. With a few steps, you can get your relationship back to where it used to be. And doing so can be as easy as 1 (analyze), 2 (compromise), and 3 (energize)!

Step 1: Analyze your love life
The first step to restoring sexual compatibility is to figure out what's going on -- or not going on -- in the bedroom and why. Experts recommend delving into your love life to see if there is a reason one of you doesn't feel like making love. Is it hormonal? Is it stress? Is it because you are really angry with your partner and don't want to make love? Resentment, is the number one reason that sex drives in **relationships** get off kilter. But in the long run, you are much better off telling your partner why you are angry rather than putting him off in the bedroom. Communication is the key.

But resentment is not the only reason that your sex life may be taking a dive. If you used to really enjoy making love but now it's the last thing on your mind, you need to rule out **medications** and/or medical conditions that could be causing the change. See your doctor for an exam and any tests they think are necessary to make sure all your systems are go. If it turns out there is a problem, then getting treatment can easily put the sizzle back in your love life.

**Tip #188**
You May Live Longer
One study suggested that married women who climaxed more often had a slight tendency to live longer. Researchers aren't sure if the sex actually lengthens your life or it's just a side effect of a healthy lifestyle. But why take any chances?

## Tip #189
Make yourself feel sexy.
Do some stretching and deep breathing, take a shower, and make the time to pick out clothes that make you feel beautiful, comfortable, and sexy. This way, when you see each other you will be relaxed, feeling super, and it will turn them on to see you so confident.

## Tip #190
Physical activities that exercise the heart are good for your health, and this includes sex. Being sexually aroused increases heart rate, with the number of beats per minute peaking during orgasm. Men, in particular, have been shown to benefit from the effect of sex on the heart. A **study** published in the AMERICAN JOURNAL OF CARDIOLOGY, involving men in their 50s, suggested that men who have sex at least twice per week have a 45 per cent reduced risk of **heart disease**, compared with men who have sex less frequently. The **American Heart Association** say that heart disease should not affect your sex life. **Heart attacks** or chest pain caused by heart disease rarely happen during sex and, for the most part, it is safe to have sex if your heart disease has stabilized.
The heart's response to sex is comparable with mild to moderate effort encountered in daily activities, according to **research** published in the EUROPEAN HEART JOURNAL. If you can take part in activities that have a similar impact on the heart - such as walking up two flights of stairs - without chest pain, then you can usually assume that it is safe to have sex.

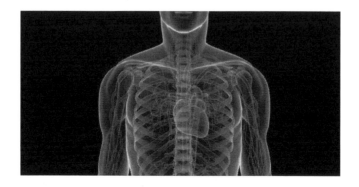

### Tip #191

Here's one of the steps you can take to destroy your husband's manhood...

Ignore him sexually (or just go through the motions). Sex matters. And many husbands are dying on the inside, wishing their wives understood how much it really does matter.

If your husband is like most, he wants a wife who is not only sexually available, but also sexually enthusiastic. If this is a big struggle for you, figure out why. And then do something about it.

### Tip #192

May Cure Your Headache

Say goodbye to the old standby **"Not tonight, Dear. I have a headache."** It turns out sex can help with pain, and that includes some kinds of headaches, such as migraines. Not feeling frisky? Try: **"Not tonight, Honey. I have a highly contagious stomach bug."** Works every time.

### Tip #193

The Power of a Good Kiss

Before you even get into the sex side of things, we are going to have to learn how to kiss. For many, a kiss can make or break it, because there's nothing quite as dissatisfying as kissing someone who doesn't kiss the way you kiss. Are you more about lips? Less about a tongue? Does kissing gross you out? Does the person just like tasting your molars? Should you floss more?

Whatever you and your spouse feel about kissing, you can do better than what you are doing. Many times we fight for our partners to conform to our way of kissing while trying to get a rhythm that works for you both. Most of the time though our attempts at manipulating the situation fall flat. We even pull away and make a joke, a little **"oh, you kiss differently from me"** comment in the hopes that they'll pick up on your not-so-subtle subtlety. Hoping that you've made your feelings about the scenario clear, you go for round two but again, you end up fighting a losing battle.

You try and you try, but are forced to realize that when someone is set in their **kissing style ways**, it's nearly impossible to break them of their habit, just as it is for them to break you of yours.

### Here's how you can do it:
1) Your lips should lock.
2) Your tongues give each other just the right amount of attention as opposed to feeling like you're having your tonsils examined, and there's magic. It's as if the world is moving right along with just how in sync you are.
3) You should kiss for a while just to see if your husband or wife still has it for you!

## Tip #194
### Dress the Part

When was the last time you brought a pair of pajamas? When was the last time you felt sexy? Are you wearing stuff to bed that no longer fits? Do you expect your partner to get dressy for you but you won't get dressy for them? When both of us value our sex life together we come to bed prepared. Maybe it would be nice to take a trip to your favorite lingerie store and find things that your partner would love to see on you!

## Tip #195
### Schedule time together.

You're going to want to plan a time that works for both of you, and not just expect your partner to follow along because you feel like romancing them tonight. Have a discussion first about wanting to take a day off (or a few hours if that's all you've got) with them. You can let them know your availability and ask them if it jives with yours. Then make a plan so you're not left in your underwear and penniless until your next paycheck. Set up a time and a place; they will appreciate it and you will both have **time to fantasize about the fun you're about to have**.

## Tip #196
### Boosts brain power

**Research** published in the Archives of Sexual Behavior suggests that frequent sex may improve women's memory. Results from a computerized word-memory task found that women who had penetrative sex had better memory recognition of abstract words.

The researchers note that at this stage, it is unclear whether sex improves memory or if better memory leads to more sex. However, they say that sex may improve memory by stimulating the creation of new neurons in the hippocampus - the region of the brain that is involved in learning and memory.

Another **study**, by the University of Amsterdam in the Netherlands and published in Personality and Social Psychology Bulletin, found that thinking about love or sex has different effects on our brains. Thinking about love activates long-term perspective and global processing, which promotes creative thinking and interferes with analytical thinking. However, in contrast, thinking about sex triggers short-term perspective and local processing, which then promotes analytical thinking and interferes with creativity.

## Tip #197
### Lowers Stress

People who have more sex are less anxious when they're faced with stressful tasks like public speaking or arithmetic. Stress can be harmful to our physical health. Yet science suggests there are natural ways to regulate anxiety. In one study, researchers found **daily intercourse for two weeks led to cell growth in the hippocampus, the part of the brain that keeps stress levels under control**.

In another study, **people who had daily intercourse for two weeks showed lower stress-related blood pressure** than those who chose to fool around in other ways or abstain from sex altogether. And more good news: The body also releases oxytocin (aka the love hormone) when two become one— it acts as a natural sedative and can trigger feelings of compassion.

### Tip #198
Practice self-love.
First and foremost, it starts with you feeling good about you. You can **tap into that through any method that works**: Taking a bath, spending time with friends, getting a **massage**, drinking some tea, or petting your cat. Whatever works, do it.
Because **to have amazing romantic sex** you need to romance yourself so you are coming from a good place, not a place of clinginess or need for affirming attention. That is not loving yourself, and if you have issues with being taken advantage of in relationships, it's time to learn how to stop being a doormat and get the love you want.

### Tip #199
Smell Good - A nice, clean smell can make you feel good, and that confidence boost can make you look better to your spouse! Wear clean clothes. If you work a job where you get filthy all the time, before you sit down... hit the shower!! Shower daily, and always after a workout. Find cologne, shampoo, soap, and deodorant with scents that you like and that your spouse likes. No sense in wearing something that they are not pleased with. For fresh breath, brush, floss, rinse, and follow your dentist's advice. If you wear a scent, only use a little.

**Tip #200**
Good for a Woman's Heart
Women who have sex a couple of times a week are less likely to get heart disease than those who have it once a month. Whether that's because healthier women enjoy it more often, or because it helps protect a woman's heart is unclear. You're probably already aware that heart disease is the number-one killer of women. Eating a healthy diet, and keeping your cholesterol low and sodium in check are great ways to stay on top of heart health, but so is having sex. Sex is exercise that raises heart rate and blood flow. In a study published in the *Journal of Epidemiology and Community Health*, researchers found that having sex twice or more a week reduced the risk of fatal heart attack by half.

If you need help with your marriage, call us. We have many years of experience dealing with Marriage problems and the situations that Marriage can bring us. Give us a chance of help you.
Call us at 770-256-8856.

Get our First Book,
**"The Wise Men and Woman Have Sent Me to Tell You"**

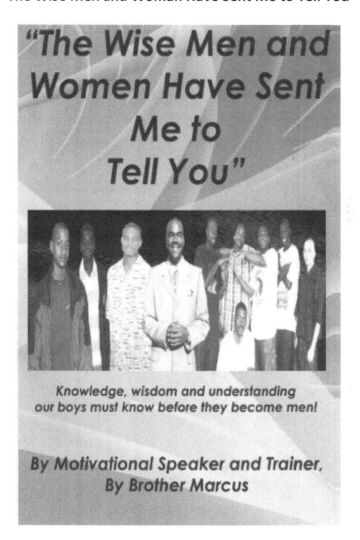

www.createspace.com/3355081

Get our Second book,
**"What do Men and Women Really Need from Each other?"**

Get our Third Book,
**"Universal Marriage and Relationship Tips" Volume #1**

Get our Fourth Book,
**"Universal Singles Tips"**

www.createspace.com/6232980

Get our Fifth Book,
**"From Courtship to Marriage"**

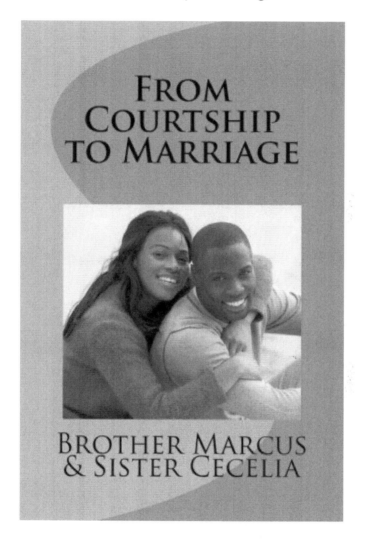

www.createspace.com/6875764

Made in the USA
Columbia, SC
09 February 2025

53558308R00067